Cambridge Topics in English Language

Language Change

Ian Cushing

Series Editors: Dan Clayton and Marcello Giovanelli

CAMBRIDGE
UNIVERSITY PRESS

University Printing House, Cambridge CB2 8BS, United Kingdom

One Liberty Plaza, 20th Floor, New York, NY 10006, USA

477 Williamstown Road, Port Melbourne, VIC 3207, Australia

314–321, 3rd Floor, Plot 3, Splendor Forum, Jasola District Centre, New Delhi – 110025, India

79 Anson Road, #06-04/06, Singapore 079906

Cambridge University Press is part of the University of Cambridge.

It furthers the University's mission by disseminating knowledge in the pursuit of education, learning and research at the highest international levels of excellence.

www.cambridge.org
Information on this title: www.cambridge.org/9781108402231

© Cambridge University Press 2018

This publication is in copyright. Subject to statutory exception and to the provisions of relevant collective licensing agreements, no reproduction of any part may take place without the written permission of Cambridge University Press.

First published 2018

20 19 18 17 16 15 14 13 12 11 10 9 8 7 6 5 4 3 2 1

Printed in the United Kingdom by Latimer Trend

A catalogue record for this publication is available from the British Library

ISBN 978-1-108-40223-1 Paperback

Cambridge University Press has no responsibility for the persistence or accuracy of URLs for external or third-party internet websites referred to in this publication, and does not guarantee that any content on such websites is, or will remain, accurate or appropriate.

....

NOTICE TO TEACHERS IN THE UK
It is illegal to reproduce any part of this work in material form (including photocopying and electronic storage) except under the following circumstances:
(i) where you are abiding by a licence granted to your school or institution by the Copyright Licensing Agency;
(ii) where no such licence exists, or where you wish to exceed the terms of a licence, and you have gained the written permission of Cambridge University Press;
(iii) where you are allowed to reproduce without permission under the provisions of Chapter 3 of the Copyright, Designs and Patents Act 1988, which covers, for example, the reproduction of short passages within certain types of educational anthology and reproduction for the purposes of setting examination questions.

Contents

Series introduction	v
How to use this book	vi
Topic introduction	vii
1 The nature of language change	**1**
1.1 The inevitability of change	2
1.2 Why study language change?	2
1.3 Approaches to studying language change	3
1.4 Why do languages change?	10
1.5 What does change mean?	10
2 A history of English	**13**
2.1 A version of history	14
2.2 The era of Old English	14
2.3 The language of Old English	17
2.4 The era of Middle English	22
2.5 The language of Middle English	26
2.6 Early Modern English	27
2.7 Late Modern English	30
2.8 Present Day English	32
2.9 The future of English	34
3 Processes of language change	**36**
3.1 How do we study language change and usage?	37
3.2 Lexical change	39
3.3 Semantic change	43
3.4 Phonological change	45

3.5 Grammatical change	51
3.6 What causes change?	55
4 Attitudes to language change	**59**
4.1 Language, politics and ideologies	60
4.2 Prescription and description	61
4.3 Metaphors and attitudes to change	67
4.4 Attitudes to phonological change	70
4.5 Attitudes to lexical change	73
5 World Englishes	**80**
5.1 Defining World Englishes	81
5.2 English around the world	84
5.3 Language contact	92
5.4 Language birth: pidgins and creoles	95
5.5 Language endangerment and death	97
5.6 Do we need global languages?	100
Ideas and answers	**103**
International Phonetic Alphabet (IPA) chart	**110**
References	**111**
Glossary	**114**
Index	**118**
Acknowledgements	**119**

Series introduction

Cambridge Topics in English Language is a series of accessible introductory study guides to major scholarly topics in the fields of English language and linguistics. These books have been designed for use by students at advanced level and beyond and provide detailed overviews of each topic together with the latest research in the field so as to provide a clear introduction that is both practical and up to date.

In all of the books in this series, we have drawn on examples of spoken and written language. We hope these will encourage you to apply the theories, concepts and methods that you will learn in the books to analyse data and to think critically about a number of issues and debates relating to language in use. Many of the books also draw on data from the Cambridge Corpus. Throughout each book, you will find short activities to help develop reading and writing skills, longer extended activities and practice questions that will enable you to explore your learning in more detail and research findings that will provide inspiration for your own language investigations. Each of the chapters includes suggested wider reading, and a full glossary and reference section at the end of each book will support you to extend your learning and provide avenues for future reading and research.

We hope that each book will give you a good overview of its topic and, that taken as a whole, the series will map out some of the most interesting and diverse areas of language study, providing you with fresh thinking and new ideas as you embark on your studies.

Dan Clayton

Marcello Giovanelli

How to use this book

Throughout this book you will notice recurring features that are designed to help your learning. Here is a brief overview of what you'll find.

> **Coverage list**
> A short list of what you will learn in each chapter.

> **KEY TERM**
> Definitions of important terms to help your understanding of the topic.

> **ACTIVITY**
> A clearly defined task to help you apply what you've learnt.

> **RESEARCH QUESTION**
> A longer task to help you go deeper into the topic.

> **PRACTICE QUESTION**
> To give you some practice of questions you might encounter in the exam.

Ideas and answers
Further information, suggestions and answers to all activities and practice questions in the book.

Wider reading
Key texts to help extend your learning.

Topic introduction

This is a book that describes the way language changes. It doesn't prescribe language use or complain about language change, but simply acknowledges that change is something that happens. It is very important to foreground this way of thinking about language, as there are many people, books and articles that bemoan language change, complaining about new words, grammatical structures and variations in pronunciation. This book seeks to challenge such views – to see language change as an exciting and interesting phenomenon to study.

At the same time, we want to try and understand *why* language changes. This involves stepping back and looking at what happens and changes around language: society, culture and context. Language doesn't just exist by itself: it is a sociocultural activity. To understand language change, we need to understand the wider contextual aspects in which language operates.

A major part of the book explores the way that people think and talk about language. This is something that is often overlooked in work on language change, but I see it as an integral part of understanding language itself. What do people think language actually is? And why do people have such strong emotions about its use, variation and change?

Chapter 1 explores some of the different approaches to language change, and focuses on how people think about language and what this means for the study of language change. Chapter 2 looks at *a* (not *the*) history of English, considering where and when the language 'began', and how it has changed over the last 1,500 years. Chapter 3 takes a closer look at the processes underlying language change, exploring the ways that words, grammar, pronunciation and meanings have changed. Chapter 4 focuses on attitudes to language, exploring people's feelings about language use, variation and change. Finally, Chapter 5 explores English as a global language, looking at how and why English is used around the world, and what this means for other societies, cultures and languages.

There is a chart of the International Phonetic Alphabet (IPA) at the end of the book to help you with the texts.

Ian Cushing

Chapter 1
The nature of language change

In this chapter, you will:

- Establish an understanding of what language change is
- Explore some approaches to studying language change
- Start to examine some of the ways English has changed and the reasons for these changes

1 Language change

1.1 The inevitability of change

All languages change over time. They always have done, and they always will. Some people find this a source of disappointment and frustration, and many have spent time trying to resist and challenge language change, complaining about imaginary things such as a 'decline in standards' and 'new, unwanted forms of language'. This is a futile endeavour, carried out by people who misunderstand what language actually is, and what it is used for. Language change is inevitable – languages are dynamic, malleable and flexible. They change in the way they look and sound, and they change in the way they are perceived by others. They have changed in the past, they are changing right now, and they will change in the future. New words come and go; languages are born, and languages die.

This book is a study of how and why those changes happen. Throughout it, you will see how English has undergone massive change over time, looking at change from both a diachronic perspective (where the historical development of a language is studied) and a synchronic perspective (where a particular moment in time is studied). In this chapter, the fundamental approaches that this book takes to the study of language change are laid out, exploring the nature of language itself and how we think, talk and feel about change.

> **KEY TERMS**
>
> **Diachronic change:** the historical development of language
>
> **Synchronic change:** the study of language change at a particular moment in time

1.2 Why study language change?

Language is a human phenomenon that both shapes and reflects the way we view and understand the world. Knowing about the ways in which language has changed can therefore offer us insight into what human behaviour is like now, what human behaviour was like in the past – and what it might be like in the future. Because language is a system for social communication, understanding how and why it has changed reveals patterns of social behaviour throughout time. As explored in this book, changes in society and changes in language are reciprocal and deeply intertwined. Understanding language change is just one of the ways that we understand society.

Figure 1.1 represents the way that language usage, variation and change are embedded within sociocultural conditions. The dotted line on the inner circle indicates the way that *language* and *sociocultural conditions* are not separate, but connected domains that influence and shape each other. So, language has

The nature of language change

different forms and functions across different sociocultural contexts such as politics and education. Context is crucial to how language works, in that it shapes how people select and use different forms, and what they do with those forms.

Figure 1.1: A sociocultural model of language use, variation and change

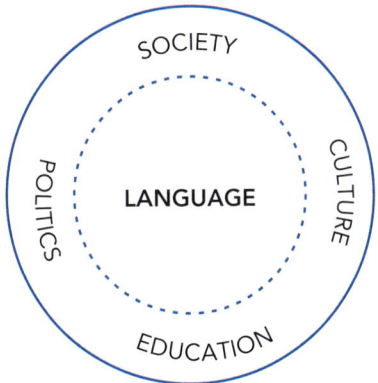

1.3 Approaches to studying language change

The next three sections outline some of the ways in which language change can be studied. These are the principles and approaches to language study that are adopted in this book, and which form an important theoretical background in terms of thinking about what language actually is.

1.3.1 Describing, not prescribing

Depending on who you talk to about language change, you are likely to encounter different opinions on whether it is a good or a bad thing – or just a 'thing' that happens, which is the view that most linguists take. Many public discourses on language change can be rather negative – it can be fairly rare to hear people say things like 'I love this new word I heard my teenage daughter say' or 'Isn't it brilliant that people don't always use punctuation marks in text messages?' Despite language change being progressive, innovative and creative, some people's attitudes towards change can be rather conservative. Many views about language are often tied up with wider aspects of society such as nationalism, traditionalism and the maintenance of moral standards.

This book adopts and advocates a descriptivist approach to language study. You will find out more about this in Chapter 4, but it is important to briefly consider what this means here, as it has direct implications for how we understand

1 Language change

language itself. **Descriptivism** is about exploring, analysing and describing language. It draws attention to how language is actually used by people in society, acknowledges language change as an important thing to study, and celebrates multicultural/multilingual diversity. For descriptivists, no language, accent or dialect is 'better' than another one – all varieties are equal in status and understood according to the context in which they appear. Descriptivists reject the notion that language choices can be either 'correct' or 'incorrect', and think about a scale of linguistic *appropriateness* instead.

This is in stark contrast to **prescriptivism**, which is concerned with hierarchical notions of linguistic standards, correctness and rules. Prescriptivists tend to bemoan language change as they often align it with 'falling standards', 'laziness' and 'sloppiness' with little regard for the actual contexts in which language occurs. For example, consider the following quotation from Norman Tebbit, a former Conservative MP who, when interviewed on the *Today* programme in 1985, suggested that there was a correlation between the ability to use 'good English' (whatever this might be), personal hygiene and a life of crime:

> If you allow standards to slip to the stage where good English is no better than bad English, where people turn up filthy at school [...] all these things tend to cause people to have no standards at all, and once you lose standards there's no imperative to stay out of crime.

As explored further throughout this book, attitudes towards language change are very rarely just about language.

KEY TERMS

Descriptivism: an approach to language study that seeks to describe language use, variation and change, where no judgement or negative attitude is imposed on language

Prescriptivism: the notion that language should be fixed, prescribing to a set standard of rules for language usage, with any shift away from these rules or standards being seen as incorrect

ACTIVITY 1.1
Discussing and evaluating language change

In groups, discuss the following statements (a–i). They are designed to provoke, so try and explore multiple points of view in your discussions. How far do you agree with each of them, and why? Why do you think some of the statements might be seen as controversial? Can you talk about them in terms of prescriptivism and descriptivism?

a. We should embrace and celebrate language change.
b. Language change is ruining the beauty of the English language.
c. If we all spoke one language, things would be a lot easier.
d. Slang and swearing should be banned in schools.
e. Technology is the main driving factor behind language change.
f. Young people are responsible for language change.
g. There is a proper and correct way to use English.
h. Bad grammar makes people look uneducated.
i. British people have a right to say how English is used because they own the language.

1.3.2 Language change as a sociocultural process

This book takes language to be a sociocultural phenomenon. This means that language has primarily a *social function*, and any study or description of language should consider the social, cultural and contextual factors in which it occurs. Understanding language in this way appreciates the fact that it is a human activity, and that changes in a language come about because of changes in human behaviour.

When exploring language from a sociocultural perspective, we can do so at different 'levels', as outlined in Table 1.1. This is a useful approach to take because it allows linguists to 'zoom in and out' to the different components of language, whether they are 'small' parts like particular grammatical constructions, or 'bigger' parts like entire **speech communities**.

Table 1.1: Levels of sociocultural processes (adapted from Culpeper and Nevala, 2012: 383)

	Level of sociocultural process	Descriptive focus	Associated descriptive focus	Brief example involving the history of English
Macro (sociological) ↕	Macro	Sociocultural structures associated with broad speech communities	For example: ideologies, cultures, nations, laws	The eighteenth-century ideology of correctness, prescriptivism and standards

1 Language change

	Level of sociocultural process	Descriptive focus	Associated descriptive focus	Brief example involving the history of English
↕ Micro (linguistic)	Mezzo	Sociocultural activities associated with local communities	For example: social practices, activity types, genres, roles	Lectures, school lessons, debates, discussions
	Micro	Sociocultural actions and reactions amongst individuals	For example: speech acts, interactions	Evaluative language, directives
	-	Linguistic forms	For example: modal verb, rising intonation, double negative	Any linguistic construction that has undergone change

The notion of a **speech community** is an important one in studying language change. The term is used to describe any socially or regionally defined human group, identifiable by the way that its members use a language (such as English) or a variety of a language (such as South London English). Most people are members of multiple speech communities, each of which have their own distinct linguistic characteristics. For example, somebody could be a member of the British English speech community, the Indian Hindi speech community and the Lancashire dialect speech community at the same time. Speech communities do not exist in neatly defined containers that bear no influence on each other – they are networks that cross over, interact and influence one another. A speech community is also broadly defined by the value or attitude towards language that it holds.

> **KEY TERM**
>
> **Speech community:** any socially or regionally defined group in which its members share a number of linguistic characteristics

Identity and language

Language is an inherent part of your identity: the way you use language signals to the world who you are, much in the same way that your clothes and taste in music do. So, one of the most important factors involved in language change is derived from its function as a social identity marker. Members of speech communities and social groups exhibit certain ways of marking group membership, lifestyle choices and cultural preferences: clothes, taste in music, ways of behaving, political views, and, crucially, language. Language is one of the key factors that marks different social groups – as well as helping to define who we are as individuals and as group members, it also helps to mark us out as different to other groups. For example, ethnographic research by the sociolinguist Anna-Brita Stenström (2014) found that certain forms of teenage language were characterised by the following linguistic features:

- irregular turn-taking
- overlaps
- indistinct articulation
- word shortenings
- teasing and name calling
- verbal duelling
- slang
- taboo lexis
- language mixing (or code-switching).

The use of such language enables teenagers to define themselves as a social group, and to distance themselves from groups that they might not want to be associated with – adults, or young children, for example. At the same time, different groups want to establish their own identity and so 'pull away' from teenage groups, in patterns of variation that create diversity and change. Young people in particular are often seen as the instigators or, as Penelope Eckert (2011: 367) describes them, the 'movers and shakers' of language change. Various researchers, including Eckert, argue that some of the motivations behind adolescents' linguistic choices and behaviour are:

- they are free to challenge linguistic norms and perceived standards
- they have a desire to build and maintain individual and group identities
- they have a desire to be seen as credible, modern and fashionable by their peers
- they seek to belong to a group that is distinct from their parents and other adults.

1 Language change

> **KEY TERM**
>
> **Code-switching:** when speakers of two (or more) different languages switch from one to the other, often in mid-conversation depending on who they are talking to or what they wish to accomplish. Can also be used to refer to switching between dialects in the same language

> **ACTIVITY 1.2**
>
> **Speech communities, identity and change**
>
> Think about the different speech communities that you belong to. For each one, consider the way that you use language within this community. What things are different and similar? Can you account for these similarities and differences? How do these factors contribute to your overall sociolinguistic identity?

1.3.3 Metaphor and language

In this book, metaphor will be used as a tool for analysing the way people talk and think about language. Metaphor is a powerful and pervasive aspect of language, which has long been recognised as a feature of everyday speech, as most famously demonstrated by George Lakoff and Mark Johnson (1980). When people use metaphor, it allows them to understand one thing in terms of another, reflecting the way that we perceive, think and talk about things in the world. For example, English is often talked about as if it were a 'living thing'. Expressions such as *the English language is alive and well*, *English has grown enormously*, *the birth of English* and *English is unlikely to die anytime soon* are all metaphorical — English has not literally 'grown' or 'been born', but is often talked about as if it had. This is metaphor.

> **KEY TERM**
>
> **Metaphor:** the use of figurative language, where one thing is understood in terms of another thing

Linguists use a recognised formula to label metaphor use in language, as in the conventions of conceptual metaphor theory. This is done by using small capital letters, in a X IS Y structure. So, the examples above can be captured through the metaphor:

ENGLISH IS A LIVING THING

In this metaphor, knowledge from conceptual 'domains' (ENGLISH and LIVING THING) are brought together in a process known as 'mapping'. This cross-domain mapping is shown in Figure 1.2.

Figure 1.2: Cross-domain mappings for ENGLISH IS A LIVING THING

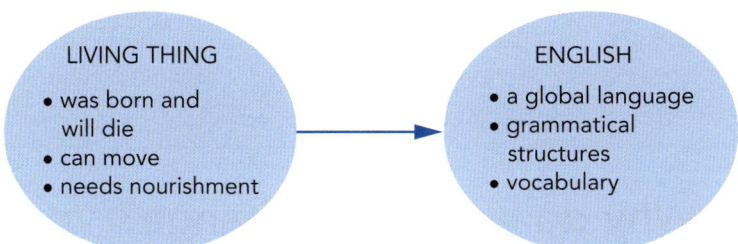

When we use metaphor, we map knowledge from one domain (the source domain) onto another (the target domain). The source domain for LIVING THING includes information that a speaker knows about things that are alive: the fact that they were born and will die, need nourishment to survive, and so on. This information is mapped onto the target domain of ENGLISH, which includes information that a speaker knows about the English language: the fact that it is a global language, has certain grammatical structures, a vocabulary, and so on.

What do you think of the ENGLISH IS A LIVING THING metaphor? Does talking and thinking about language in this way affect the way you actually understand what 'language' is? Lakoff and Johnson argue that metaphor does not just *reflect* the way we see the world, but *constitutes* it. If this is true, then what does this mean for the way we talk – and think – about language?

There are various other ways of talking and thinking about language through metaphor, which will be returned to throughout the course of this book. In addition to the LIVING THING metaphor, Mario Saraceni (2015) also suggests how the metaphors of LANGUAGE IS A TRAVELLER and LANGUAGE IS A PHYSICAL OBJECT are often used to talk about the way that English has 'moved', 'spread' and 'grown' across the world. These metaphors are highly commonplace, giving rise to expressions such as *English has arrived here*, *the English language taken to India* and *we must protect the English language*. He argues that such expressions project a rather simplified understanding of what language is, and fail to include any kind of human agency or involvement. Languages do not just exist by themselves: there are always speakers and often ideological motivations for wanting to 'cut down', 'spread' and 'grow' a language. Saraceni suggests that the metaphor of LANGUAGE IS AN OPEN SOURCE CODE offers a useful way of thinking about how language is a network of features that can be accessed, modified and enhanced by its users.

In this book, language will be understood through a different metaphor: that is, LANGUAGE IS AN EVENT. This metaphor is chosen to try and capture the way that language is *not* a physical object, but is an abstract concept controlled and

Language change

adapted by people who use it in different sociocultural contexts. It also tries to capture the dynamic and ongoing nature of language change.

> **KEY TERM**
>
> **Conceptual metaphor:** a theory of a metaphor whereby one 'domain' of knowledge is 'mapped onto' another domain. The convention for writing conceptual metaphors is through the use of small capitals, in an X IS Y structure

1.4 Why do languages change?

We have seen that language change is inevitable, ongoing and happening right now. But why? This is a difficult question which has no simple answer – the causes of language change are various and only some of them are reasonably understood. It may be useful to think not of 'language changing' but instead of 'people changing language'. Re-conceptualising language change in this way positions human beings as the subject of the verb *changing*, emphasising the 'force' and agency of the speakers behind language.

Language change is natural, and deliberate attempts to either trigger or stop it have been met with fierce resistance, and almost always failed. Despite a number of efforts to 'fix' and standardise a language, or to purposefully introduce new reforms (such as the alternative, phonetic-based English spelling system proposed by the Simplified Spelling Society), English has continued to change and exist without the need for restrictive interventions.

Deep social changes are the main reasons for changes in a language, and the English language is a reflection of the history and lives of the people who speak it. This point cannot be stressed enough: political, economic, social and cultural factors are powerful forces that influence the way a language is used and changes. Such changes manifest themselves in different ways, whether it be a shift in the way a word is pronounced, a new word that enters into a language, or a speaker in a different country shifting to a new language. Chapter 3 explores the processes of language change in further detail.

1.5 What does change mean?

Depending on who you talk to, you are likely to encounter different opinions and attitudes towards language change. Some people are inclined to view changes in a language as 'sloppy' or 'lazy', whereas other people regard new forms as perfectly normal. It is absolutely *not* the case that changes are symbolic of a

The nature of language change

'decline' in the language or of 'falling standards'. Indeed, if all of the changes that have happened to English in the last 1,500 years had been a drop in standards, then modern English would surely be so crude that we would hardly be able to use it at all.

A related argument is made by Jean Aitchison (2012), who suggests that language change is indicative of progress, rather than decline. Most of the people who bemoan language change are concerned with linguistic purism, a zero-tolerance approach to change with the view that one variety of a language is inherently better than another, and that change somehow means language deterioration.

KEY TERM

Linguistic purism: a pejorative label used for a view that sees a language as needing preservation from things that might make it change, such as dialect variation and borrowings from other languages

RESEARCH QUESTION

Eliciting views on language change

Design a set of interview questions, prompts or statements about language change, which seek to address some of the issues raised in this chapter. These might include things like:

- How do you define 'correct' spelling, punctuation and grammar? Is it always necessary to use these correct forms?

- Is there anything about the way that English is used that irritates you?

- Which social groups do you think are the most responsible for changes in the English language, and what is your attitude towards this?

Once you have your questions, put them to as wide a range of people from different social groups (e.g. teenagers, grandparents) as you can. Once your data is gathered, compare the responses across groups, which will give you more data to explore. What do your comparisons reveal about people's attitudes and feelings about the nature of language change?

1 Language change

Wider reading

Read more about the nature of language change from a sociocultural perspective by exploring the following books:

Aitchison, J. (1991, reedited 2012). *Language Change: Progress or Decay?* Cambridge: Cambridge University Press.

Fennell, B. (2001). *A History of English: A Sociolinguistic Approach*. London: Blackwell.

Leith, D. (1997). *A Social History of English*. London: Routledge.

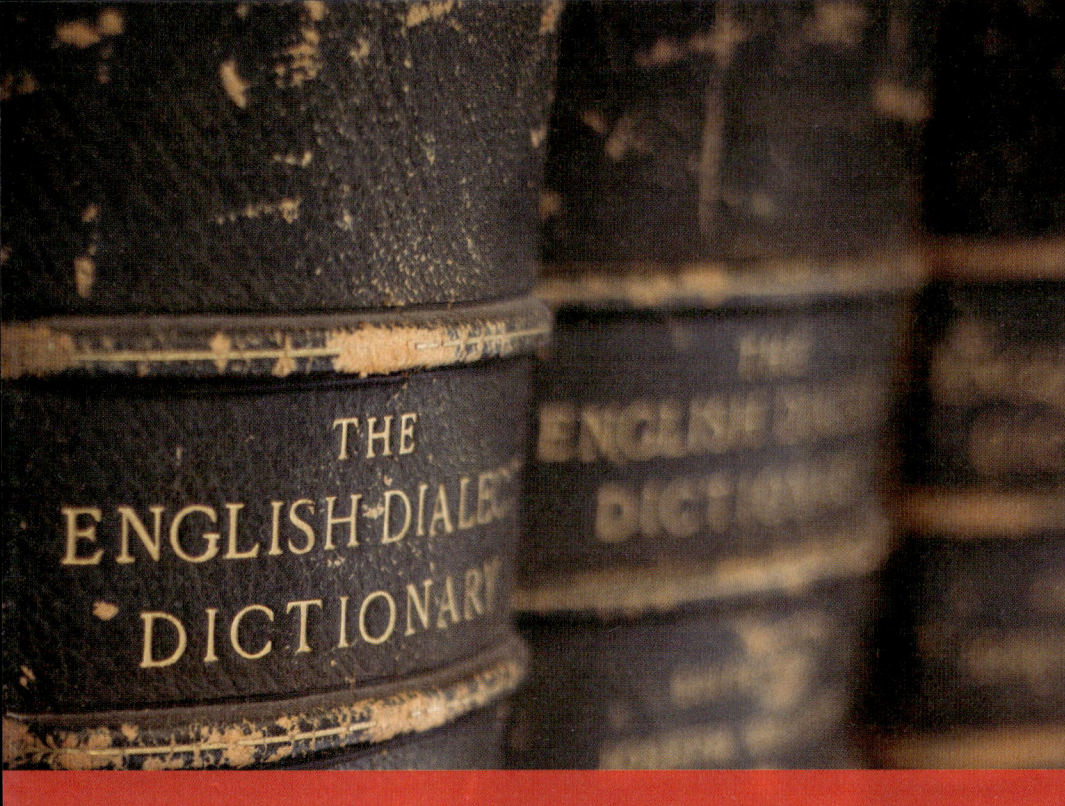

Chapter 2
A history of English

In this chapter, you will:

- Consider the development of English over time
- Examine some of the historical and social factors that have led to language change
- Explore some of the ways in which English has changed

2 Language change

2.1 A version of history

This chapter is called *a* history of English rather than *the* history of English. It is not *the* definitive history of English, as any history of events can be told in an infinite number of ways. Different histories of English will tell you different things – for example, one version may celebrate the colonial expansion of the British Empire and the subsequent rise of English as a global language, whereas another may despair at the way English has killed off other languages as its use expands across the world. A prescriptivist version may lament the way English changes, but a descriptivist version will seek to understand the reasons behind change. This particular history attempts to present events not as 'facts' but as one possible version of a long and complicated story. Charting the history of a language is a challenging puzzle – linguists play detective in piecing together information to try and form a picture of what languages used to look and sound like, and the causes that triggered change.

In Chapter 1, it was argued that language is primarily a *sociocultural* phenomenon. This is important to keep in mind when thinking about and studying language change. Languages change because society changes, not of their own free will. The story of English is bound up with massive societal changes in terms of wars, invasions, inventions, colonisation, conflict, globalisation, and billions of different human voices. This means that language change does not happen in a neat way, with all changes conveniently falling within particular time scales and being easily accountable for. However, certain patterns of language change have allowed linguists to formulate historical linguistic eras. This chapter looks at each of these in turn. They are:

- Old English (OE) 449–1100

- Middle English (ME) 1100–1500

- Early Modern English (EME) 1500–1800

- Late Modern English (LME) 1800 – present day

- Present Day English (PDE) (present day onwards)

Remember that change is gradual – it doesn't happen overnight, and because of this, dates given are often estimates.

2.2 The era of Old English

We begin this history of English in 449AD, with the arrival of a group of Germanic invaders to Britain. Before their arrival, the lands we now call Britain were mostly home to Celts who spoke various Celtic languages such as Welsh, Scottish Gaelic, Irish, Cornish and Manx. The invaders were made up of a number of different groups: Jutes, Saxons and Frisians. These groups spoke a number of closely related varieties of Germanic languages, and collectively they came to think of their speech as English, with dialects reflecting the heritage of each different group. Does this mean that we should think of Old English as *Old Englishes* instead? Perhaps. Indeed, an often simplified version of English history downplays the enormous amount of regional variation during this time, construing 'English' as one resource that was used in the same way across speech communities. A more accurate view would be that right from the very beginnings of English(es), we see examples of language contact, a process of change whereby multiple languages meet and influence each other. Language contact can trigger conflict and sociocultural uniformity in equal measure, but the result is always some kind of linguistic change.

It must be noted that linguistic data from this 'birth' of English is completely unavailable. The first attempt to document the history of this era comes from a source published nearly 300 years after the invasion of 449AD, in the form of *Historia Ecclesiastica Gentis Anglorum*, written in Latin by the monk Bede. This means that any history of English – including this one – includes some guesswork. These issues should be taken into account when thinking about language change over time.

KEY TERMS

Language contact: a process of language change whereby multiple languages come into social contact and have linguistic influence on each other, in the form of borrowings, grammatical and phonological change, formation of **pidgins** and **creoles**, and higher rates of multilingualism

Pidgin: a language that develops between two speech communities who do not share a common language

Creole: a language that originally began as a pidgin, and has become the mother-tongue of a speech community, with its own native L1 speakers

2.2.1 Missionaries and Latin

In 597AD, a group of Christian missionaries arrived in Britain from Rome, bringing the influence of the Latin language with them, including the Roman alphabet. These missionaries were led by St. Augustine who successfully converted the Anglo-Saxon ruler, King Ethelbert, in a matter of months. Christianity soon took hold in Britain, adding new words from religious contexts into English such as *monk*, *nun*, *pope*, *candle* and *priest*. And yet, despite its growing influence as a religion, Christianity was largely confined to the educated classes, who were able to access the Latin language in which much of the texts were written, and in which sermons were spoken.

2 Language change

2.2.2 The Vikings

In the late eighth century, Britain found itself once again under invasion, this time by Vikings from Denmark, Norway and Sweden. A high number of raids took place until the beginning of the eleventh century, and an agreement was eventually forged between the Viking king Guthrum and the English ruler of Wessex, Alfred. This agreement – known as the Danelaw – saw Britain divided in two, with the Vikings ruling the North and the East, and the Anglo-Saxons ruling the South and West, marked by a road between London and Chester. The Vikings spoke Old Norse, a North Germanic language, which gradually became part of the English language as the interaction between speech communities increased. Most Norse words that were 'borrowed' into English during this time were related to administration, law, Old Norse and the military. This is perhaps not surprising, given the ongoing tensions between the Vikings and Anglo-Saxons, as each group tried to wrestle control of the borders set out by the Danelaw.

Figure 2.1: Map showing the division of Britain under the Danelaw

2.3 The language of Old English

Are Old English (OE) and Present Day English (PDE) really the same language? To illustrate, look at Figure 2.2, which shows the front of Franks Casket, a box dating from the early eighth century. At the top, bottom and left of the box you will see a series of runes – an alphabetic system used for carving in wood or stone, and widely used throughout the Germanic world.

Figure 2.2: Franks Casket

Is this really the same language as PDE? Texts such as these were much closer linguistically to European and Scandinavian languages than what the successor to OE – Middle English – ended up looking like, so it perhaps seems a little odd that these texts are referred to as 'Old English'. Here, it is important to note that the etymology (the study of the origin of words) of the term 'Old English' is a politically motivated one, introduced by historians who wanted to create the idea that the English language had an inflated sense of longevity, ancient history and rich tradition. James Milroy (2002: 19) calls this the 'myth of the ancient language', a term used to try and describe the long 'journey' that English had come on, in an attempt to conjure up a sense of linguistic nostalgia and tradition. Even so, when the runes are transliterated into the Roman alphabet, they still make very little sense to a twenty-first century user of PDE (see Text 2A).

2 Language change

Text 2A

Fisc flodu ahof on fergenberig;

warþ gasric grorn, þær he on greut giswom.

Hronæs ban.

Mægi.

The flood lifted up the fish on to the cliff-bank;

the whale became sad, where he swam on the shingle.

Whale's bone.

Magi.

Transcription and translation of runes on Franks Casket

Although the Roman alphabet was used for writing (rather than the runes in Figure 2.2), the linguistic 'distance' between the kind of English found in Text 2A and contemporary usage provides a clear idea of just how much languages can change over time. To reiterate a point made in Chapter 1, it is important not to see older varieties of English as somehow inferior to the current version. Languages do not change for the 'better' or for the 'worse', and OE was still just as expressive and flexible as PDE. It had slang, regional and personal variation, taboo lexis, informal and formal registers, and just as many other linguistic variables as are found in PDE. You will explore more about attitudes to change in Chapter 4.

ACTIVITY 2.1
Old English detective

Read **Text 2B**, a short extract from *De Temporibus Anni* (The Seasons of the Year), an OE text by the monk Ælfric, from around 993AD. Are there any linguistic characteristics (words, letters, grammatical classes, syntactical constructions, etc.) from PDE that you recognise in this text? What do your findings tell you about how English has changed? What kinds of things from OE might have remained? Complete the activity before reading any further. To get you started, the text begins like this: 'On the fourth day God created the two lights that are the sun and moon…'

A history of English

Text 2B

> On ðam feorðan dæg gesceap God twa miccle leoht þæt is sunne and mona and betæhte þæt mare leoht is seo sunne to ðam dæge and þæt læsse leoht þæt is se mona to ðære nihte. On ðam ylcan dæge he geworhte ealle steorran and tida gesette. On ðam fiftan dæge he gesceop eal wyrmcynn and ða micclan hwalas and eal fisccynn on mislicum and menigfealdum hiwum.
>
> Extract from *De Temporibus Anni*

There are some recognisable elements in Text 2B, such as the prepositions *on* and *to*, the auxiliary verb *is*, and the conjunction *and*. This is very typical of what remains in PDE; much of the OE influence lies in these kinds of short function words. Function words (prepositions, certain auxiliary verbs, conjunctions and determiners) are much more resistant to language change because they are the 'nuts and bolts' of the linguistic system and, as such, are less susceptible to change. Changes in vocabulary items usually occur in lexical words (nouns, adjectives, verbs and adverbs). Chapter 3 looks at this in more detail. Indeed, the only instantly recognisable lexical word in Text 2B is a noun: *God*. In the following sections, you will explore some of the written, phonological, lexical and grammatical characteristics of OE. The aim here is not to provide a full description of these, but to illustrate some of the key features and how they fit into the wider picture of language change. Full descriptions can be found in Barber et al. (2012) and Smith (2005), amongst others.

2.3.1 Writing system and pronunciation

One of the reasons that Text 2B looks so alien to a modern English reader is because of the writing system. The spelling system reflected the phonology of the time, and goes some way to illustrating how the language was pronounced during this period.

- OE used the Roman alphabet, introduced by missionaries. This gradually replaced the runic system.

- Although many letters were the same as PDE, the letters <j>, <k>, <q>, <v> and <z> were hardly ever used.

- The OE letters <ð>, <þ> and <æ> are no longer used. <ð> and <þ> have been replaced by <th>, and <æ> by <a>.

- <ρ>, called 'wynn', was later replaced by <w>.

- Because the spelling system was not yet standardised, and was written down phonetically, OE had no 'silent' letters. So, the initial consonants of words such as *cnapa* (servant) and *wrītan* (write) were pronounced, as were initial consonant clusters *hwǣr* (where) and *hwīt* (white), and medial <h> in words such as *niht* (night). All vowels were pronounced.

Language change

- The OE vowel system distinguishes between long and short vowels. The vowel inventory was /y, i, e, æ, a, o, u/, with a short and long version of each phoneme.

- Sometimes <c> was pronounced /tʃ/ and <g> as /j/.

- The consonant clusters <sc> and <cg> were pronounced /ʃ/ and /ʤ/, respectively.

> **KEY TERM**
>
> **Writing system:** a method for visually representing spoken language, including letters of alphabets and punctuation marks

2.3.2 Lexicon

The OE lexicon consisted of words inherited from its Germanic ancestors and words 'borrowed' from other languages which it had come into contact with, such as Greek, Latin, French and various Scandinavian languages. Many borrowed words are related to Roman technology and religion, reflecting the social context of the time. New words were also formed through compounding and affixation – processes covered in more detail in Chapter 3.

2.3.3 Grammar and syntax

The principle difference between OE and PDE is that OE was an inflected language. In PDE, relationships between words are largely expressed by word order; in OE, these relationships are expressed by the endings of words, known as inflections. PDE still retains *some* inflections, such as possessive and plural endings on nouns (e.g. *Eve/Eve's* and *bicycle/bicycles*), and pronouns also change depending on whether they appear in Subject or Object position (e.g. *she loves him* not *she loves he*). OE had a fairly complex inflection system that we describe in terms of case, agreement, number and gender.

- Case is a grammatical category related to the morphology of nouns, pronouns, determiners and adjectives, and the role they play in a phrase or clause. OE had four cases:

    - Nominative (the form of the word in Subject position)

    - Accusative (the form of the word in Direct Object position)

    - Genitive (used to express possession)

    - Dative (the form of the word in Indirect Object position, within a preposition phrase).

A history of English

- Agreement is related to the way word forms correspond to others. For example, OE nouns agree with the determiner that precedes them, and are assigned the appropriate case ending:

    Se hlaford bindeþ þone cnapan

    The lord binds the servant

    (example taken from Smith 2005: 52)

    Here, *se hlaford* (the lord) is the Subject in the nominative case; *þone cnapan* (the servant) is the Direct Object in the accusative case. There are two forms of the determiner *the*: (*se* and *þone*). These are different because they are modifying nouns in different cases.

- Number refers to whether a word is singular or plural. Whereas PDE generally indicates number on nouns by adding an '-s' ending and by changing forms of the pronoun (e.g. *this* vs. *those*), OE grammar also indicates number on determiners and adjectives.

- Gender markings can be one of three types: masculine, feminine or neuter. PDE has no gender markings apart from on pronouns (e.g. *he*, *she* and *it*) and possessive determiners (e.g. <u>*her*</u> book/<u>*his*</u> book). In OE, the gender category determined the morphological properties of the word. Gender assignment was arbitrary – in other words, there is not always a direct or intuitive form-meaning pairing. For example, *wīf* (wife) is grammatically a neuter gender; *cudele* (cuttlefish) is feminine and *stān* (stone) is masculine. The loss of grammatical gender was one of the large-scale changes in the history of English, labelled 'the Great Gender Shift' by Poussa (1992).

KEY TERMS

Case: a grammatical category related to the morphology of nouns, pronouns, determiners and adjectives, and the role they play in a clause or phrase

Agreement: the way that word forms correspond to and 'agree' with others

Number: grammatical marking indicating whether a word is in the singular or plural form

Gender: a grammatical or semantic category of words, showing contrast between masculine, feminine or neuter

2 Language change

Now we move on to look at OE verbs:

- OE verbs could be in either present or past tense, as is the case in PDE.

- They could be in three moods (sometimes referred to as modality), referring to the different degrees of possibility they can express: the indicative (for statements and questions), the imperative (for commands), and the subjunctive (for wishes and hypotheticals). We use the subjunctive much less in PDE, although it did have a revival in British English during the second part of the twentieth century.

- Verbs could be strong or weak. Strong verbs form the past tense by changing the vowel (such as present tense *sing* vs. past tense *sang*). Weak verbs form the past tense by morphological inflection, for example by adding –d (such as present tense *dance* vs past tense *danced*).

Finally, because of the number of inflections in the grammar, OE syntax displayed a much more flexible word order than PDE allows for. PDE has a Subject-Verb-Object (SVO) word order, whereas OE had the following options (where C stands for Complement): SVO, SVOC, CSVO, VOC and VOCS. Over time, OE gradually lost its inflections and word order became more fixed. After the Norman Conquest in 1066, English became heavily influenced by French, which had a rigid word order but few inflections. This meant that OE's capacity for having free word order was lost.

> **KEY TERM**
>
> **Mood/modality:** a system of meaning related to a speaker's attitude to, confidence in, or perception about something in the world

2.4 The era of Middle English

Middle English (ME) is the term used to describe the varieties of English used between approximately 1100 and 1500. We have access to far more written material from this era than OE, as English remained the primary choice of language for native speakers and was eventually adopted by the Norman-French invaders, who arrived in 1066. Despite the long-lasting influence of French, the status of English during this era grew to one of high prestige, further establishing itself as an important part of national identity.

2.4.1 The Norman invasion

In 1066, the English language was changed forever. When the king of Wessex, Edward the Confessor, died in 1060, he appointed Harold Godwinson as his successor, but William of Normandy contested his claim to the throne. This

A history of English

dispute led to the Norman invasion of Britain and, in 1066, William was crowned the first Norman King of England, becoming William the Conqueror. The Normans spoke Old-Norman (which gradually changed to *Anglo-Norman*), a dialect of French, which itself is a Romance language derived from Latin. Following his ascension to the throne, William was faced with English rebellions. He exiled the English rebels and rewarded his supporters with lands and the offices of the English nobility. Thus, the English – and the English language – began to lose prestige, being replaced by Anglo-Norman. High status roles were taken by the Normans, while English remained the language of the lower classes.

2.4.2 Diglossia, variation and contact

This sociolinguistic shift can be described as diglossia: where one or more languages (in this case, Anglo-Norman, French and Latin) assumes the role of 'high status' variety, being used for state and religious purposes; and one language (English) fulfils the role of 'low status', used largely in informal speech circumstances. Regional variation in ME was high: there was no regulation on English in the form of grammars or dictionaries, no standard variety, and the language was rarely written down, further threatening its status. The future of English looked bleak. And yet, despite French rule for over 300 years, the English language survived, primarily because of the huge numbers of native speakers who only spoke English. Over time, the English and Norman languages merged, as natives and Normans married and became socially closer.

KEY TERM
Diglossia: a term mostly used in sociolinguistics, referring to a situation where two very different varieties of a language exist alongside each other, each holding a distinct social function

ACTIVITY 2.2
Attitudes to Middle English diglossia

Read Text 2C, and then answer the questions (a–d). This text was written in the late thirteenth century by Robert of Gloucester. For the purposes here, it has been translated into PDE. 'William the Bastard' refers to the Norman invader; 'Harold' refers to the king of England at the time of the invasion.

a. What attitudes towards diglossia are presented in the text?

b. Imagine you were (i) a Norman invader and (ii) a native English speaker. How might you feel about diglossia, taking into account each sociolinguistic identity?

2 Language change

c. Why do you think people felt so strongly about language during this time?

d. What do such attitudes reveal about the way language is tied up with nationalism, nation-building and identity?

Text 2C

Much sorrow has been often in England,
As you may hear and understand,
Of many battles that have been and men have conquered this land.
First, as you have heard, the emperors of Rome.
Then the Saxons and Angles with battles strong,
And then those of Denmark that held it so long,
At last those of Normandy that be yet here
Won it and hold it yet; I will you tell in what manner:

When William the Bastard heard tell of Harolds' treachery,
How he had made him king and with such falsehood,
For that land was given to him, as Harold well knew
...
Thus came – lo! – England into Norman's hands,
And the Normans could not speak anything except their own speech,
And spoke French as they did at home, and their children did also teach,
So that high men of this land that of their blood come
Hold to all that speech that they took of them;
For unless a man knows French, men think little of him.
But low men hold to English and to their own speech yet.
I suppose there be none in all the countries of the world
That do not hold to their own speech, save for England alone,
But yet it is well for a man to know both,
For the more a man knows the more he is worth.

Extract from *The Chronicle of Robert of Gloucester* (c.1300)

2.4.3 The rise of English

While the ME period is noted for French influence on social and linguistic structures, the end of this period saw notions of 'Englishness' emerging and a growing sense of pride in the national language. Events such as the creation of the Magna Carta in 1215 transferred legal power to those who previously had little, and took power away from those who had too much (such as the monarchy and social elite). The Hundred Years' War (actually from 1337 to 1453) between England and France positioned the French language as 'the enemy', further promoting the idea that nationhood and language are closely related. The Black Death in 1348 diminished the rural population so much that they could demand better working conditions and move to areas that offered better prospects, which saw the rise in geographical mobility and social status of the peasant classes who were fiercely proud of the English language. The year 1362 saw the passing of the Statute of Pleading, decreeing that English be the language of the law courts. In 1384, John Wycliffe produced a translation of the Bible in English, challenging the status of Latin as the language of religions. By 1385, English was the chosen language of education in schools. By the end of the fourteenth century, literature was produced in both French and English, and notable writers such as Geoffrey Chaucer opted to use English for their works, reflecting the growing sense of English linguistic identity.

ACTIVITY 2.3
Translating Middle English

Read through Text 2D, an extract from *Sir Gawain and the Green Knight*, written in the English of the late fourteenth century. To the best of your ability, try and produce a modern-day translation. Once finished, use your translation to help you analyse the original. What do you notice in terms of the writing system, vocabulary and syntax? How does this differ from Old English? For example, the first line could be translated as:

In a strange region he scales steep slopes

Text 2D

Mony klyf he ouerclambe in contrayez straunge,

Fer floten fro his frendez fremedly he rydez.

At vche warþe oþer water þer þe wyʒe passed

He fonde a foo hym byfore, bot ferly hit were,

2 Language change

> And þat so foule and so felle þat feȝt hym byhode.
>
> So mony meruayl bi mount þer þe mon fyndez,
>
> Hit were to tore for to telle of þe tenþe dole.
>
> Sumwhyle wyth wormez he werrez, and with wolues als,
>
> Sumwhyle wyth wodwos, þat woned in þe knarrez,
>
> Boþe wyth bullez and berez, and borez oþerquyle,
>
> And etaynez, þat hym anelede of þe heȝe felle;
>
> Nade he ben duȝty and dryȝe, and Dryȝtyn had serued,
>
> Douteles he hade ben ded and dreped ful ofte.
>
> Extract from *Sir Gawain and the Green Knight*
> (Anonymous, late fourteenth century)

2.5 The language of Middle English

2.5.1 Writing system and pronunciation

- Spelling was still not standardised, and there remained a high amount of variation.
- The OE letters <ð>, <þ> and <æ> gradually fell out of usage. <þ> was retained the longest. OE <ȝ> was retained in some texts, or replaced by <g>.
- The Norman <qu> replaced Anglo-Saxon <cw> in words such as *cwene* (*queen*).
- The /ʃ/ sound gradually became represented as <sh> rather than <sc>.
- Word-initial <hw> became <wh>.
- Word-initial <h> was gradually deleted, in words such as *hnecca* (neck).
- The writing-sound system remained phonetic, with all letters being pronounced.
- Many long vowel sounds were written with a double vowel, such as *se* changing to *see*.
- ME saw a significant increase in the number of diphthongs, when compared against OE.

2.5.2 Lexicon

ME is characterised by language contact, and so acquired a high number of borrowings. The main sources of these were French and Latin.

- French borrowings number in their thousands, and reflect the kind of social change occurring during England at the time. Most were nouns. Words were borrowed from categories as diverse as government/administration (e.g. *chancellor*, *crown*, *state*, *treason*); religion (e.g. *saviour*, *sermon*, *theology*, *virgin*); law (e.g. *attorney*, *justice*, *slander*); military (e.g. *army*, *combat*, *enemy*); food (e.g. *bacon*; *beef*); clothing (e.g. *cape*, *jewel*, *plume*) and culture (*grammar*, *painting*, *music*).

- Borrowings directly from Latin tended to be more formal words, e.g. *allegory*, *contempt*, *gesture*, *necessity* and *testimony*. Many of these borrowings introduced new affixes into English:

    - suffixes: *-able, -ible, -ent, -al, -ive*

    - prefixes: *ab-, ad-, am-, ante-, con-, dis-, im-, in-, pro-, re-, sub-*.

2.5.3 Grammar and syntax

ME is much easier for PDE readers to understand because of the loss of many inflections.

- Nouns, determiners and adjectives were no longer marked for grammatical gender, and verb endings were reduced in variety.

- Most case endings largely disappeared, especially the nominative, accusative and dative case. As a result of this, word order became fixed, losing the flexibility offered by OE.

- English word order was established as Subject-Verb-Object.

- Pronouns retained their gender, number, person and case distinctions.

2.6 Early Modern English

Early Modern English (EME) is bookended by two important events: the arrival of printing technology in England in 1476 and the publication of Samuel Johnson's *A Dictionary of the English Language* in 1755. Both of these changed the way that English was written. Because writing is much less liable to change, English underwent an increased process of standardisation, where the language became more uniform. Literacy rates increased as a result, triggering huge social change and greater access to culture. Britain increased its international trade activity, bringing

Language change

words from various world languages into English, as contact was made around the world. Also of enormous significance during this era was the Act of Union in 1707, which formed the state of Britain between England, Scotland and Wales. This Act triggered the beginning of the British Empire, projecting the English language and its people around the world. By the end of the twentieth century, English was one of the dominant languages of the world.

> **KEY TERM**
>
> **Standardisation:** the process under which a language develops a standard 'prestige' variety

2.6.1 Literature

Between the sixteenth and eighteenth centuries, a flurry of creative activity saw a rise in literary works written in English in what is known as the 'golden age' of English literature. Writers such as John Donne, Andrew Marvell, John Milton and William Shakespeare all opted to use English, rather than Latin or French, which had previously been the languages of choice for the social elite and the educated classes. What impact did this have on the English language? First of all, it meant that attitudes towards the language shifted to more positive ones, with English taking on an increased sense of gravitas and social status. Secondly, vocabulary size increased as writers created new word forms and experimented with word meaning, with thousands of words from over fifty languages entering into the language. Shakespeare himself introduced hundreds of words, phrases and idioms that are still in use today (Crystal 2004), as well as experimenting with the syntax of English in highly creative ways. And finally, the increase in written publications helped to standardise the language.

2.6.2 Printing, dictionaries and grammars

Another reason why there was a surge of published literary works during this era was because of printing technology, which was brought to England in 1476. The man responsible for this was William Caxton, who published a range of literary works from his London printing press. The location of the press was important – Caxton published using the dialect, grammar and spelling system of the capital city. This helped to promote the idea of a 'Standard English' – a kind of benchmark or reference point to which all other varieties of English were compared. There was a growing sense of the need for English to be 'regulated', and for linguistic uniformity. It follows that the most important objects in this era of English were dictionaries: records of the language which presented a standard model of English, with a regular spelling system. Two of the most influential dictionaries are owed to two men, Cawdrey and Johnson:

- In 1604, Robert Cawdrey published the first English dictionary, *A Table Alphabeticall*, consisting of around 3,000 short entries. Cawdrey intended his dictionary to be useful for 'Ladies, gentlewomen, or any other unskilfull persons, whereby they may more easily and better understand many hard English words'.

- In 1755, Samuel Johnson published his *Dictionary of the English Language*, consisting of 40,000 detailed entries. Although Johnson had initially set out to 'fix' what he saw as the chaotic and unruly variation in English spelling, he eventually recognised that language is ever-changing, and conceded that his role was to describe English, rather than prescribe it.

As well as dictionaries, many grammars of English were published in the seventeenth century. The most influential of these was Robert Lowth's *A Short Introduction to English Grammar* in 1762 and Lindley Murray's *English Grammar* in 1794. Around 200 grammars were published during the EME era, most of which were highly prescriptive, arguing for a 'correct' way of using English and presenting themselves as a kind of 'linguistic manual'. The rise of prescriptivism was accentuated by people such as Jonathan Swift and John Dryden, who called for the creation of an 'English Academy' – a group to decide on correct usage and 'protect' the language from falling into disrepute.

2.6.3 The Great Vowel Shift

A major development in English phonology took place across the fifteenth and sixteenth centuries, known as the Great Vowel Shift (GVS). During this time, the sounds of the long vowels in English changed their places of articulation. Essentially, vowels shifted to a different point of articulation in the mouth, in a process of language change generally referred to as a chain shift. This means that when one sound changes it has a knock-on effect on other sounds. The changes are listed in Table 2.1 (adapted from Smith 1999: 131).

Table 2.1: The Great Vowel Shift

Word	ME vowel sound	PDE vowel sound
life, bite	[iː]	[aɪ]
meet	[eː]	[iː]
meat	[ɛː]	[iː]
gate	[aː]	[eɪ]

2 Language change

Word	ME vowel sound	PDE vowel sound
how, town	[uː]	[au]
mood	[oː]	[uː]
boat	[ɔː]	[oʊ]

Quite what triggered the GVS continues to be debated. Linguists have theorised a range of potential factors, such as: an influx of loanwords from other languages; high death rates during the Black Death which caused geographical population changes; and changes in perceived social status of vowel sounds. Given the growing sense of language and regional identity, it is likely that people hypercorrected their pronunciation to try and indicate their status. Whatever the reason(s) were, the GVS gave rise to many of the peculiarities of English pronunciation that we have today. Whilst some spellings changed to reflect the change in pronunciation (e.g. *barn* from *bern* and *heart* from *herte*), many did not. So, in PDE we have multiple spellings for one vowel sound (such as the [uː] in *due*, *chew* and *too*), and one spelling for multiple vowel sounds (such as the <ea> in *knead*, *bread*, *wear* and *great*).

> **KEY TERMS**
>
> **Chain shift:** a situation where a series of sound changes take place, with each one influencing the next
>
> **Hypercorrection:** an over-emphasis shift in linguistic register, usually when a speaker of a non-standard variety goes 'too far' in trying to emulate the standard variety

2.7 Late Modern English

From 1800 onwards, the English language accumulated more speakers and a larger vocabulary. Two of the contributing factors to this were growth in other areas: industry and the British Empire. The next sections explore how and why these had an impact on English.

2.7.1 Industry

The British Industrial Revolution was a period of great technological change, lasting from around 1760 to 1840. Tasks previously done by hand were gradually automated and performed by machines, with a rise in mass production, transport technology and standards of living. New inventions meant that new words and phrases were needed, so we see terms from semantic fields such as fashion (e.g. *mackintosh*, *rubber*), technology (e.g. *telephone*, *camera*, *electricity*), science and medicine (e.g. *cholera*, *oxygen*, *vaccine*) and transport (e.g. *train*, *engine*, *piston*) from this era. A spin-off of industrial revolution is urbanisation, resulting in greater population densities – and increased levels of language contact.

2.7.2 Colonialism and the British Empire

Between the late sixteenth and twentieth centuries, the British Empire took the English language throughout the world, and brought foreign words back to England. The Empire reached far and wide, with colonies in Egypt, the Americas, Canada, Ireland, Singapore, Nigeria, South Africa, India, Australia, New Zealand, the West Indies and many others. Figure 2.3 is a map of the world in 1907, with British colonies outlined in red. English was imposed as an official language in many of these colonies, with the British invaders often showing little respect for local indigenous languages. Where large numbers of native speakers existed, such as in India, English was established as the second language. For the colonisers, imposing English as a language was an important way of establishing authority, with the language deployed as a political tool for wrestling control of new lands and demonstrating power. Speakers of English are often guilty of seeing themselves as at the top of a hierarchical linguistic ladder, where their access to and use of English offers them rights over those who speak other languages. This is known as linguicism (Skutnabb-Kangas, 1988) or linguistic imperialism (Phillipson, 1992), which will be explored further in Chapter 4. The English language has a violent and somewhat sinister past, rather than the often jingoistic way in which 'the Empire' and the global growth of English is celebrated and reminisced about. Given this sociocultural context, there are a number of metaphors that we might use to reflect the way English changed at this time: ENGLISH IS A POLITICAL TOOL; ENGLISH IS A STEAMROLLER and ENGLISH IS A BULLY.

KEY TERMS

Linguicism: a term used to draw parallels between hierarchies on the basis of race or ethnicity, gender and language

Linguistic imperialism: an ideological view and process of language change, whereby one language is imposed on speakers who use another language, often undermining the rights of those speakers. It promotes the idea that there is a hierarchy of languages

2 Language change

Figure 2.3: The British Empire in 1907

2.8 Present Day English

Present Day English (PDE) refers to any one of the varieties of English currently spoken around the world. As will have become clear through this chapter, it perhaps does not make sense to speak of 'one English' but 'many Englishes', each with its own unique linguistic characteristics. Given the massive amount of variation across these Englishes, just a few of the key features are presented here:

- PDE continues to change, most noticeably with the arrival of new vocabulary and meanings (e.g. *Brexit, babyccino, drunk text, superfruit, climate* and *freecycle*, all of which have become popular in recent years).

- Borrowings and phonological and syntactical patterns continue to be adopted from a wide range of cultures, reflecting the process of twenty-first-century globalisation and language contact.

- Technology has influenced the way we use language, particularly in relation to multi-modal communication such as social media and computer tools.

- In the UK, regional accents continue to display diversity and innovation.

- English continues to be used around the world and is widely regarded as the international language of trade, education and the internet.

A history of English

- English continues to be seen as a prestigious and desirable global language.
- English is seen as responsible for the extinction of less commonly spoken languages, a topic explored in more detail in Chapter 5.

With the affordances that computer tools and the internet offer, English usage is now widely documented. Many universities host corpora of language – huge databases of spoken and written speech. Some of these can be explored for free, such as the British National Corpus (www.cambridge.org/links/esccha6001). Academic journals such as *English Today* and *English Language and Linguistics* publish on contemporary usage and record the way that English is changing. With these huge databases of language at their disposal, linguists can now explore how language is used on a much larger scale, without relying solely on a narrow snapshot of data.

> **KEY TERM**
>
> **Corpora:** (plural of corpus) large databases of a language, used for research purposes and to document the way that a language is used and changes

ACTIVITY 2.4
Metaphors of English

Using your knowledge of the way English has changed over time, explore the meaning of the following metaphors (1–10). Consider what each metaphor might mean in relation to the way the language has changed and adapted, thinking about what kind of information is mapped onto ENGLISH in each example. What 'kind' of English is construed in each one? Which metaphor do you think best reflects English, and why? What linguistic expressions might fall under that metaphor? Finally, can you think of other metaphors to describe English? Some suggestions have been made for the first one.

(1) ENGLISH IS A FAST-FLOWING RIVER

This metaphor reflects the idea that English has a strong Germanic identity (the main river), but exists in a network of connections or 'tributaries'. For example, English has been enriched by vocabulary from Scandinavian languages, Norman French, Latin, Greek and others. You might also think of these tributaries as the various regional and global varieties of English (explored further in Chapter 5). Change has happened quickly and steadily, much like the way water moves in a rapidly flowing river. There may be rapids or waterfalls, reflecting high density of change in certain periods such as the Industrial Revolution.

2 Language change

There are no dry parts of the river, reflecting the constant change that English has undergone. The river reaching the sea could reflect the global status and size of English, with other oceans representing other global languages such as Spanish and Arabic. Expressions that fall under this metaphor would be things such as:

the <u>flow</u> of English is <u>coming quickly</u>
English <u>sprang</u> from a small <u>source</u> and is now <u>an ocean</u> of a language
the change in English is unlikely to <u>dry up</u> anytime soon

(2) ENGLISH IS A CONTAINER

(3) ENGLISH IS A SPONGE

(4) ENGLISH IS A CURRENCY

(5) ENGLISH IS A WEAPON

(6) ENGLISH IS A SPIDER WEB

(7) ENGLISH IS A PIECE OF CLAY

(8) ENGLISH IS A FOREST FIRE

(9) ENGLISH IS A BUSINESS

(10) ENGLISH IS A MAGPIE

2.9 The future of English

Language change is messy, complex and largely unpredictable. In this chapter, you have seen how change in a language is an inevitable consequence of change in society. This means that English *will* continue to change in the future, despite efforts by prescriptivists and self-proclaimed 'defenders' of the language. It will not get 'better' or 'worse', and, once again, it is important to steer clear of such adjectives when thinking and talking about language.

A history of English

RESEARCH QUESTION

What does the future hold for English?

There is a range of websites and resources that try to predict the future of English. Using the internet, explore what some of these sources say. A good place to start is www.cambridge.org/links/esccha6002. Think about:

- What view of English do the writers have?
- What metaphors do they draw on when writing about language?
- Do you agree with the way that English is talked about? Why/why not?
- How is the view of language tied up with views around nationalism and patriotism?
- Finally, do you think we can ever predict the future of a language? Why/why not?

Wider reading

Read more about English and its various histories by exploring the following books:

Barber, C., Beal, J. & Shaw, P. (2009). *The English Language: A Historical Introduction*. Cambridge: Cambridge University Press.

Phillipson, R. (1992) *Linguistic Imperialism*. Oxford: Oxford University Press.

Smith, J. (2005). *Essentials of Early English*. London: Routledge.

Watts, R. (2011). *Language Myths and the History of English*. Oxford: Oxford University Press.

Chapter 3
Processes of language change

In this chapter, you will:

- Examine some of the main ways that the English language has undergone change
- Consider why and how language changes
- Reflect on some of the ways that language continues to change

Processes of language change

Chapter 2 introduced some of the sociocultural contexts surrounding the 'story' of English, and identified some of the ways that this has shaped the way the language has changed. This chapter looks at the *processes* of change: in other words, the specific ways in which English has changed. It considers etymology and lexical change: where new words come from, how they are formed, and how their meanings change over time. It will also look at phonological change, in how the sounds of English have changed. Finally, the process of grammatical change is explored, and some of the attitudes towards this.

Once again, there will be an emphasis on the idea that language change and variation is not arbitrary, but exhibits patterns that are driven by sociocultural changes.

3.1 How do we study language change and usage?

We all know that languages change – but how do we monitor this? In the past, linguists would often draw on tools from anthropology and archaeology to help them uncover the histories of a language, piecing together evidence from written texts. Although this approach is still valid, linguists today often make use of corpus linguistics. This method makes extensive use of corpora and computational tools to document and study language change and usage; an approach that provides a number of advantages in examining how a language develops over time. Corpora are large collections of texts (often consisting of more than a million words), which can then be searched and analysed using computers. Figure 3.1 is a screenshot of the *Cambridge English Corpus*, showing the surrounding words for the phrase 'English is a'. Looking at the results, what things strike you as interesting?

> **KEY TERMS**
>
> **Etymology:** the study of the origin of words and the way they change in meaning
>
> **Corpus linguistics:** a method of studying language using computational tools and big datasets (corpora)

3 Language change

Figure 3.1: Extract from the *Cambridge English Corpus*

```
d be an interesting day. Texican </p><p> English is a mongrel tongue. It is basically composed of 29
                                     and now -are English is a bonus. </p><p> Hopefully, they will still be tak
e's more patient with colleagues for whom English is a second language. But the big change, and hard
revisers of dissertations, writers for whom English is a second language, or authors of manuscripts tha
1. Laboy, a native of Puerto Rico for whom English is a second language, passed the test, including dict
 Latin or Greek roots. </p><p> In origin, English is a Germanic tongue based on the Germanic dialect
blic access web sites, web users for whom English is a second language and on-line advertisers. He sai
ed, working, works , and so on. </p><p> English is a , deriving originally from Anglc
  for Best Speech By A Politician For Whom English Is A Second Language. Despite the many nominatior
 o lag behind in reading; children for whom English is a second language; and special-needs students. A
those with disabilities and those for whom English is a second language? </p><p> Which schools or d
11 teachers, who teach children for whom English is a second language. </p><p> The national union
:onomy and society. Strong competence in English is a great advantage in order to enter and graduate
es, can be intimidating for those for whom English is a second language. </p><p> "A lot of people are
 quotations or as unconscious borrowings. English is a West Germanic language originating in England
bsolutely "brillean"! Thay you are teaching English is a worry... </p><p> If " in no way condones
ise applicants must speak and understand English is a form of illegal discrimination based on national
tive teachers of English in countries where English is a foreign language, coupled with a growing conce
ii-Deitsch Children learn English in school. English is a West Germanic language originating in England
 ... </p><p> The King's English The King's English is a quaint, independent bookshop in the 15th and 1
oup according to their particular traditions English is a West Germanic language originating in England
merican English within American English . English is a pluricentric language , without a central languag
ich more useful and easy it is. </p><p> " English is a most noble and melodious tongue as one hears
```

Another useful (and free) tool for doing corpus linguistics is Google Ngram, an online database of written texts published between 1500 and 2008. You can access it here: www.cambridge.org/links/esccha6007. Ngram allows you to compare the usage of multiple words or phrases against each other over time. For example, Figure 3.2 is a screenshot from Ngram comparing the words *philology* and *linguistics*. *Philology* is the traditional term for the study of language, but came to be replaced by *linguistics* in the 1950s, a time when there was a surge of interest in the discipline. Here then, is a nice, clear example of a social change impacting on language change. Activity 3.1 asks you to explore Ngram for yourself.

Figure 3.2: Corpus linguistics with Ngram

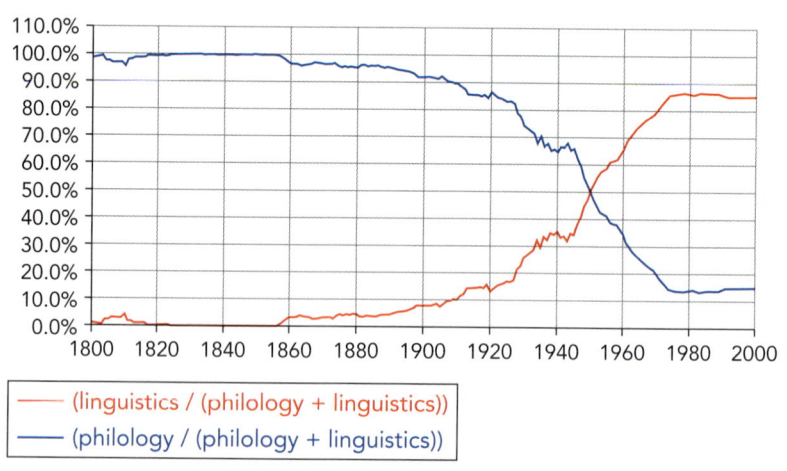

Processes of language change

ACTIVITY 3.1
Doing corpus linguistics

A revealing way of studying language change on Ngram is to compare multiple words or phrases against each other. This can be done by simply separating lists of words by a comma. So, where WORD A and WORD B are the two words to be compared:

> WORD A, WORD B

for example:

> *philology, linguistics*

Try the following searches for yourself. You could try predicting what the result will be before you search, and then discuss the potential reasons for the results. As you do this, think about sociocultural changes and what you learnt about some of the historical issues of English in Chapter 2.

- *motor car, car*
- *courting, dating*
- *wireless, radio*
- *analogue, digital*
- *policeman, policewoman*
- *letter, email, fax, telegram*
- *pavement, sidewalk*
- *correct grammar, incorrect grammar, bad grammar, good grammar*

Finally, using word groups of your own choice, explore their usage distribution.

3.2 Lexical change

In any language, the most audibly and visually noticeable change is the appearance (and disappearance) of new words. You may well remember the first time that you heard a new word, including where you heard it, who used it, and what your reaction was like. When new words enter a language, it is called the process of lexical change.

3 Language change

Jean Aitchison (2012) suggests that once a new word has been identified, this can trigger the process of lexical diffusion, whereby its usage is gradually taken up by a speech community. It can take time for a new word to filter through the language – and some new words simply don't take hold. However, if and when a word gains currency through widespread use by a variety of people and in different contexts, then it becomes established, with its meaning and pronunciation gradually becoming more uniform.

> **KEY TERM**
>
> **Lexical diffusion:** the increased use of a linguistic form throughout an area over a period of time

Lexical expansion takes place for two main reasons:

- **Need:** as people's social and cultural experiences expand, they need a vocabulary that reflects and allows discussion about these new experiences.
- **Contact with others:** the increased ability to travel, including immigration and resettlement, has seen the incorporation of new words and phrases from other languages into the English lexicon.

There are various different types of (and reasons for) lexical change, which are examined in turn below.

3.2.1 Borrowing

Borrowing is the incorporation of features (typically vocabulary) of one language into another. The term itself seems rather misleading, given the implication that the speakers of a language take a word for a limited amount of time before returning it to the original source – which does not happen. A more accurate term might be *replication* or *copying*, since the original term 'lives on' in the source language. Aitchison (2012: 142–143) lists four important characteristics of borrowing:

1. The kinds of elements that are borrowed are easily detachable from the source language and will not affect the structure of the borrowing language. Vocabulary items are borrowed with ease, without any kind of limit. For example, French gastronomy words such as *gâteau* and *sorbet* were readily borrowed into English because of the sense of perceived prestige and sophistication.

2. Borrowed items tend to adapt to fit in with the structure of the borrowing language. For example, Russian speakers borrowed words from English and

Processes of language change

then adapted them to reflect the phonological properties of their language: *dzhemper* for *jumper* and *dzhaz* for *jazz*.

3 A language tends to borrow items from another language which appear to resemble features of its own. For example, language contact on the French-German border has resulted in the French language adopting certain syntactical characteristics of German.

4 The borrowing language makes a series of minimal adjustments to its internal structure, rather than huge leaps at once.

The metaphor ENGLISH IS A SCAVENGER has often been used to describe the way that English has borrowed extensively from other languages. Some of the points of contact between English and other languages were explored in Chapter 2, which is the main reason for the high amount of borrowings in English. Figure 3.3 gives an idea of the sources of the thousands of words that have been 'loaned' to English.

Figure 3.3: Borrowings in English

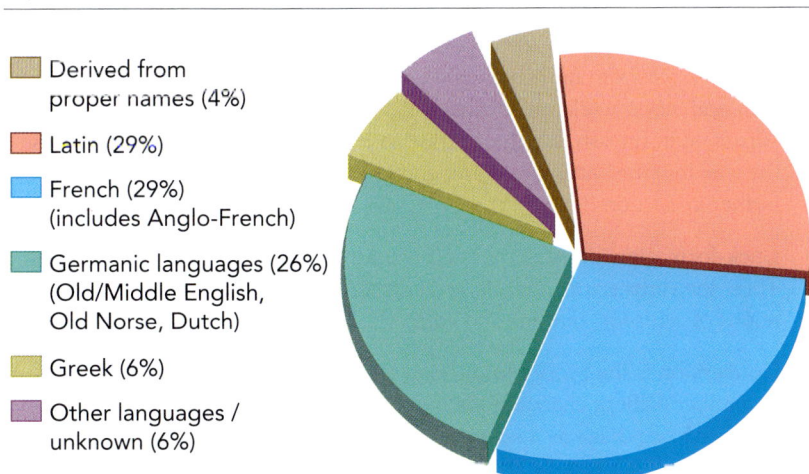

- Derived from proper names (4%)
- Latin (29%)
- French (29%) (includes Anglo-French)
- Germanic languages (26%) (Old/Middle English, Old Norse, Dutch)
- Greek (6%)
- Other languages / unknown (6%)

3.2.2 Word formation

If new words are not taken from another language, then speakers will form new ones, in a process called word formation. There are various different ways that this process happens, some of which are explored here.

- **Compounding** is an extremely common process of word formation, where two or more existing words combine to create a new word. Examples include: *ice cream*; *lipstick*; *jetlag*; *girlfriend*; *toothbrush*; *environmentally friendly*; *nevertheless*, *daydream,* and so on.

3 Language change

- **Clipping** is where an existing word is shortened, retaining the original meaning. For example, *telephone* is clipped to *phone*; *gymnasium* becomes *gym*, *antifascist* becomes *antifa* and *celebrity* becomes *celeb*. Words can also be shortened through the process of acronyms, whereby the first letter of each word in a phrase is taken to form a new word, such as *RAM* (*random access memory*) and *AIDS* (*acquired immune deficiency syndrome*). Initialisms are where the first letter of words in a phrase are each pronounced separately: *BBC* (*British Broadcasting Corporation*) or *FBI* (*Federal Bureau of Investigation*), for example.

- **Blending** is a combination of compounding and clipping, where parts of an existing word combine to form a new word. Well-known examples include *smog* (*smoke+fog*) and *brunch* (*breakfast+lunch*). More recent examples include *Brexit* (*Britain+exit*), *broflake* (*brother+snowflake*) and *staycation* (*stay+vacation*). Although blending is a highly creative method of word formation, many blends tend to be rather transient and fail to take hold in popular usage.

- **Affixation** (or derivational morphology) occurs where words 'multiply' into new ones, using affixes (either prefixes or suffixes). Thus, prefixes such as *inter-*, *anti-* and *poly-* can be glued onto existing words to generate new meaning: *internet*; *anti-establishment*; *polymath*. Suffixes such as *-less*, *-ism* and *-hood* work in the same way: *selfless*; *Britishism*; *sisterhood*. Affixation in English is highly productive, with affixes being relatively free in the way that they attach to existing words. Morphological change is covered further in Section 3.5.1.

- **Back-formation** is where part of a word that *looks* like an affix is removed. Thus, the verbs *sculpt*, *burgle* and *edit* are derived from their respective nouns of *sculptor*, *burglar* and *editor*.

- **Conversion** is the process of moving a word from one grammatical category to another without changing the morphology of the word. For example, *Facebook* began life as a noun but is now also frequently used as a verb: *I'll facebook her later*. Other (less recent) examples include the adjective *brown* being used as a verb: *brown the meat*, the verb *commute* used as a noun: *my commute to work is killing me*.

KEY TERMS

Acronym: a process of word formation, whereby the initial letters of a phrase are pronounced as a single word, e.g. NATO for North Atlantic Treaty Organization

Initialism: a process of word formation, whereby the initial letters of a phrase are pronounced as separate sounds, e.g. BBC

Processes of language change

ACTIVITY 3.2
Patterns of lexical change
Use the *Recent updates to the Oxford English Dictionary* website (www.cambridge.org/links/esccha6008) to find new words that have entered English. Pick around 20 at random, and analyse either the source of borrowing or the word-formation process, or both.

3.3 Semantic change

In this section, the notion of semantic change is explored. This is the process whereby the *meaning* of a word changes over time. English words have undergone changes in meaning for centuries – for example, in Old English the preposition *with* meant 'against' and the verb *explode* meant 'to drive out'. As with lexical change, one reason for semantic change is the sociocultural context in which language is used. Take the word *car*: this used to refer to 'a wheeled cart pulled by animals', but when technology enabled engines to replace animals, the meaning of the word shifted. There are various processes of semantic change, which are as follows.

- **Broadening** (or generalisation) is where a word 'spreads' or broadens its meaning. For example, the word *dog* used to only refer to a specific type of canine, but is now used in a much more general sense to denote all canines. In its original meaning, *rubbish* was only used as a noun, referring to 'broken stones', but is now used to denote any unwanted items, and can also be used as an adjective.

- Closely related to broadening is the notion of **semantic bleaching**, when a word's literal meaning 'reduces' in intensity. The use of the term 'bleaching' implies a lightening of meaning, where a word is deprived of vitality or substance. Many intensifying adverbs in English have undergone the process of bleaching, such as *literally*, *awfully*, *pretty* good. For example, imagine a speaker who has a cold using the phrase *I'm literally dying*. Here, *literally* is used in a very non-literal way!

- **Narrowing** (or specialisation) is where a word 'thins' or narrows its meaning. For example, *deer* and *meat* used to refer to all types of livestock and food, respectively. *Wife* in Old English has narrowed from 'woman' to 'woman of humble rank' to 'married woman'.

- **Amelioration** (or elevation) is where a word's meaning 'improves', taking on a more positive meaning. For example, *queen* and *knight* used to refer to simply 'woman' and 'boy', but are now used to denote people who hold positions of power.

43

3 Language change

- **Pejoration** is the opposite to amelioration – where a word takes on a more negative meaning. For example, *spinster* originally meant 'a person who spins (thread)', and gradually came to be used in a derogatory sense for 'unmarried woman'. *Churl*, *villain* and *boor* were once used to mean 'farm-worker' but took on negative meanings over time. Interestingly, words referring to females tend to take on pejorative meanings much more than the male equivalents. To illustrate this, consider the word pairs below (adapted from Trask 1996: 43), which once denoted 'parallel' meanings. How have they changed, and which way have they gone?

master	*mistress*
sir	*madame*
governor	*governess*
bachelor	*spinster*
working man	*working girl*

- **Metaphor** is an extremely common process of semantic change, where a word or concept is understood in terms of something else. Some metaphors are so commonplace that we tend not to even realise that they are just that. For example, take the word *head*. The original, literal meaning of this refers to the body part. As the thing containing the brain and sensory components such as the eyes, ears, mouth and nose, the head is regarded as a very important part of the body. Hence, over time, *head* has been extended and used in a metaphorical sense, to denote all kinds of people and concepts that are perceived as important, as well as the top or front parts of objects. This gives rise to expressions such as *head teacher*, *head of the table*, *head of the company* and *bedhead* (where *head* means 'top of a hierarchy' or 'most important/prominent component').

    Metaphors like this are everywhere in language: we talk about the *root* of a problem, a *bright* person, the *bottom* of the class, a *hard* exam and the *journey* of life. Indeed, most body parts can be used metaphorically: *the foot of a table*; *the eyes and ears of a company*; *a knee-jerk reaction*, and so on. As has been discussed throughout this book, we even talk about language itself using metaphor: the *seeds*, *growth* and *spread* of English; the *killing* of minority languages and the *defence* of a language.

- Closely related to metaphor is **metonymy**. This is using language in a 'part for whole' way, whereby the use of an attribute or feature of something is used to denote the thing that is being referred to. For example, using *the crown* for 'the queen', *number 10 Downing Street* for 'the UK government' or '*he's such a suit*' to mean 'he's such a corporate businessman'.

- **Taboo language** and **euphemisms** provide ways of talking about socially sensitive subjects such as sex, death, excretion and parts of the human body. In order to avoid talking about such subjects literally, speakers of a language are particularly creative in developing new words and phrases. For example, *they're sleeping together* refers to sexual intercourse, and *where's the bathroom?* can mean 'I need to urinate'.

3.4 Phonological change

Phonological change is concerned with how the sounds of a language change. Research on phonological change often relies on spelling systems, given the fact that sound recording equipment is a fairly recent invention in terms of how old English is. Linguists rely on sound *reconstruction* to study older varieties of English, using written language such as grammars, schoolbooks and poems as a form of evidence.

The following sections look at different types of sound change that arise as a result of connected speech, which is the study of how neighbouring sounds influence each other.

> **KEY TERM**
>
> **Connected speech:** a term used to refer to spoken language when analysed in a continuous sequence, including how neighbouring sounds affect one another

3.4.1 Assimilation

Assimilation is a common type of sound change, whereby two sounds become more alike. This change largely happens due to economical and efficiency reasons: when people speak, they combine vocal articulator movements in a series of complex patterns to produce different sounds, and assimilation makes the production of these sounds easier.

Partial assimilation is where neighbouring sounds *influence* each other. For example, try saying the phrase *one cause* out loud and slowly – monitor the transition point between the final consonant in *one* and the initial consonant in *cause*. What sounds are produced here? They could be transcribed as /wʌn kɔːz/. But is this actually how the phrase sounds in naturally occurring speech? In reality, it is much closer to /wʌŋkɔːz/, where the alveolar nasal /n/ moves its place of articulation backwards, assimilating to a velar nasal /ŋ/ as a result of influence from the velar plosive /k/ that follows it. For more detail on the sounds

3 Language change

of English and pronunciation, see the IPA chart at the end of this book. A more complete overview of the mechanics of speech is presented in *Text Analysis and Representation* in this series.

Total assimilation occurs when neighbouring sounds become the same. For example, in naturally occurring speech, what might happen to the /n/ consonant in the phrase *ten mice*? In many cases, /n/ would assimilate to become a bilabial nasal /m/, yielding the following transcription: /temaɪs/.

> **KEY TERM**
>
> **Assimiliation:** a process of phonological change, whereby two sounds influence each other and become more alike.

3.4.2 Lenition

Lenition (or weakening) is where a sound becomes 'weaker' along a scale. Voiced plosive sounds are at the top of this scale and are the 'strongest' sounds, in that they require the most articulatory effort and have a long constriction length. This is followed by voiceless plosives, voiced fricatives, voiceless fricatives and then approximants. Figure 3.4 shows how this can be represented on a scale:

Figure 3.4: Lenition scale

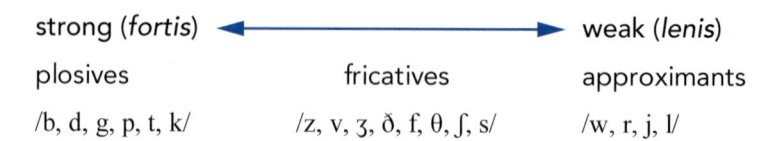

strong (*fortis*)		weak (*lenis*)
plosives	fricatives	approximants
/b, d, g, p, t, k/	/z, v, ʒ, ð, f, θ, ʃ, s/	/w, r, j, l/

Speakers generally prefer to make less rather than more articulatory effort, meaning that many consonants shift towards weak positions during speech production. A pervasive example from British and American varieties of English is tapping or flapping, which affects the articulation of /t/ and /d/. When either of these plosives occur in between a vowel, they often change to an alveolar tap /ɾ/ or a glottal stop, /ʔ/. Both /ɾ/ and /ʔ/ are still plosive sounds, but carry significantly less energy than /t/ or /d/, and so are 'weaker' sounds. An alveolar tap sound is made when there is a brief, rapid contact between the tongue and the roof of the mouth, and the plosive sound is not fully realised – hence it being a weaker sound, and moving towards the right on the scale above. A glottal stop is made when the vocal folds are tightly closed so that air cannot pass between them. Since the tongue is free during the production of a glottal stop, it is allowed to assume its position for the sound that follows – a very economical and energy-saving way of speaking.

Processes of language change

Think about how words such as *city* and *body* are pronounced in American English (which provides good examples of /t/ weakening to /ɾ/, as in /sɪɾi:/ and /bɒɾi:/). Most accents in English will feature lenition in some form or another, and although there is variation in how this is realised, /t/ is the phoneme that is generally reduced, such as in the pronunciation of *butter* in some accents: /bʌʔə/.

Lenition can also be very extreme, so that complete phonemes are omitted in a process called elision. For example, said by itself, the word *sixth* would normally be articulated as /sɪksθ/, but in a phrase such as *the sixth month*, the /θ/ undergoes elision, and would be realised as /ðəsɪksmʌnθ/.

> **KEY TERMS**
>
> **Lenition:** a process of phonological change, whereby a sound becomes 'weaker' in its articulation
>
> **Tap (flap):** a manner of articulation of consonant sounds, whereby a single, rapid point of contact is made between two vocal articulators (such as the tongue and the roof of the mouth)
>
> **Elision:** a process of phonological change, whereby a sound becomes omitted

3.4.3 Vowel reduction

Vowel reduction is a change to the acoustic quality of vowels, where typically a vowel becomes 'weaker': shorter in length, quieter and with less-defined articulation. It can be thought of as a type of lenition. When a vowel is reduced, it is often realised as the 'schwa' sound /ə/. For example, /ɒv/ often becomes /əv/ when unstressed – the 'of' in *teacher of English* would not be /ɒv/ but /əv/, to be transcribed as /ti:tʃərəvɪŋlɪʃ/.

3.4.4 Fortition

Fortition involves the 'strengthening' of a sound, where a consonant moves from right to left on Figure 3.4. It is much less frequent than lenition, given that speakers much prefer to produce sounds that require less articulatory effort than more. Fortition in English is usually realised when a voiceless plosive (either /p/, /t/ or /k/) occurring in syllable-initial position is aspirated – that is, when an extra burst of air escapes through the vocal folds, which sounds like /h/. So, words such as *party* and *appear* include aspiration on the /p/. This is transcribed using a 'small h' diacritic mark as in [pʰ].

3 Language change

> **KEY TERMS**
>
> **Fortition:** a process of phonological change, whereby a sound becomes 'stronger' in its articulation
>
> **Aspiration:** the audible breath which may accompany a consonant's articulation. It is marked by a diacritic [ʰ] as in [pʰ]

3.4.5 Sociophonetics

In the following two sections, two case studies from the field of sociophonetics, that is, research conducted at the interface of sociolinguistics and phonetics, are explored. Linguists who work in sociophonetics examine language variation and change, and the relationship between social factors such as gender, ethnicity, class and age with speaking style. Given the emphasis this book places on sociocultural factors in language change, sociophonetics is considered to be an important and exciting field of enquiry that can offer useful and revealing answers to issues in language study. *Language Diversity and World Englishes* in this Cambridge Topics series explores sociophonetic variation in further detail.

Case study of a sound change: th-fronting

In September 2016, *The Telegraph*, a UK newspaper known for its rather prescriptivist and conservative views on language, published an article with the headline '*Th' sound to vanish from English language by 2066 because of multiculturalism, say linguists*. Although it quickly transpires the headline was somewhat misleading, disparaging of diversity and factually incorrect – the /θ/ and /ð/ phonemes are, in fact, *not* going to vanish – the article nevertheless points to an interesting aspect of phonological change in English. The change in question is known as th-fronting, whereby the articulation of the dental fricatives /θ/ and /ð/ shifts forward in the mouth to a labio-dental fricative of /f/ or /v/ sound, respectively. So, *think* becomes /fɪŋk/, *mother* becomes /mʌvə/ and *bathe* becomes /beɪv/. The feature is sometimes regarded as an accent feature of non-standard, lower class, typically younger groups, and is an important marker of sociolinguistic identity, as argued by Jane Stuart-Smith and Claire Timmins (2006).

Th-fronting is a common feature of many UK accents, including parts of London (where it originally started), Essex, Sheffield and Glasgow. Figure 3.5 (from Kerswill 2003: 234) shows the diffusion of th-fronting across the UK. The dates indicate the dates of birth of speakers using th-fronting, and the size of the circles indicates the population size of each town or city. As you look at the map, you might like to think about your own pronunciation. Does your accent feature th-fronting? If so, does your hometown appear on the map? If not, then we are witnessing a 'live' phonological change in process, especially given the map is now rather out of date.

Processes of language change

Figure 3.5: Th-fronting diffusion in the UK

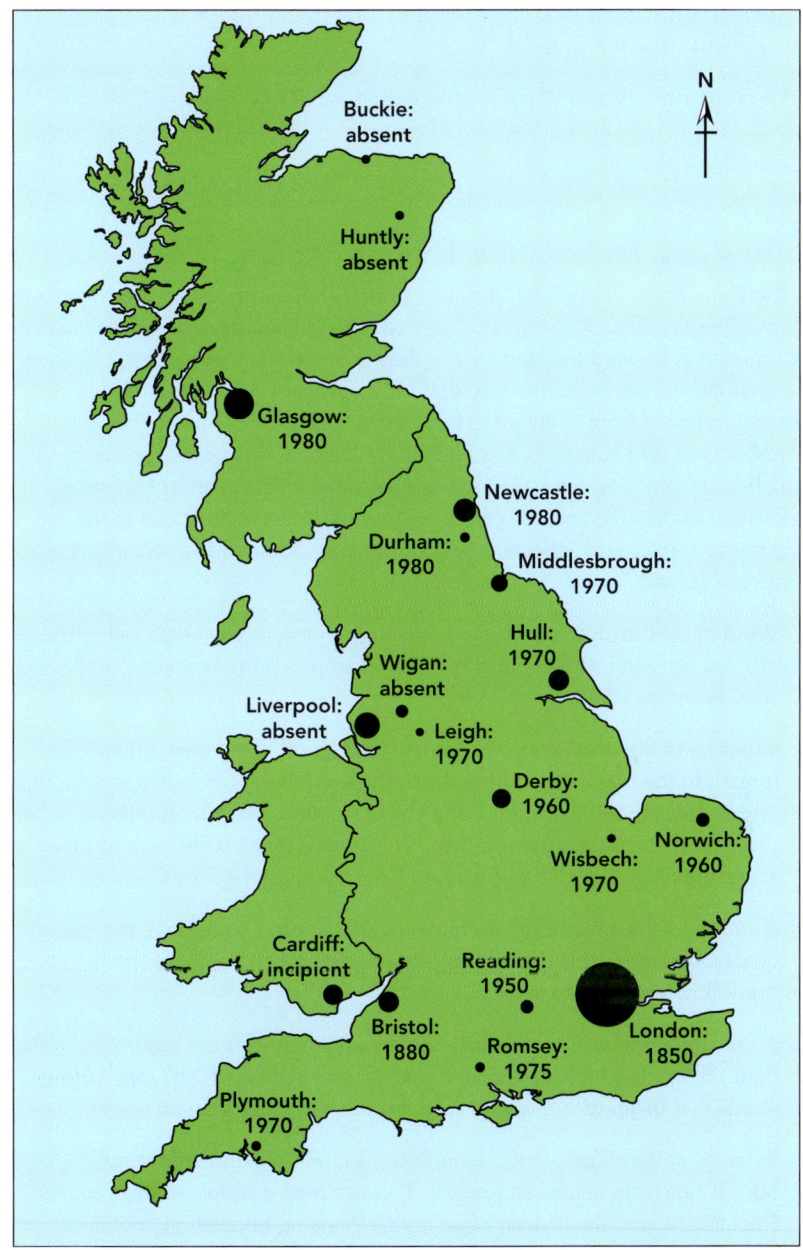

3 Language change

> **KEY TERMS**
>
> **Sociophonetics:** a branch of linguistics at the interface of sociolinguistics and phonetics
>
> **Th-fronting:** a phonological process whereby the dental fricatives /θ/ and /ð/ shift forward in the mouth to a labio-dental fricative of /f/ or /v/ sound, respectively

Case study: Multicultural London English

Multicultural London English (MLE) was primarily documented by the linguists Jenny Cheshire, Paul Kerswill and Sue Fox. These linguists describe language in a progressive, forward-thinking way as they draw on the metaphor of LANGUAGE IS A RESOURCE to talk about the way that MLE speakers use a 'repertoire of features' selected from a 'linguistic feature pool'. This pool includes various words, sounds and structures across different dialects, from which speakers can choose from. London has long been regarded as the centre of linguistic innovation in the UK, because of the amount of dialect contact due to the population density and superdiverse communities. Some of the phonological resources include:

- Word-initial th-stopping, where words that prototypically begin with /θ/ and /ð/ are replaced with /t/ and /d/. For example, *think* becomes /tɪnk/ and *they* becomes /deɪ/.

- Changes to diphthongs in /eɪ/ (*face*), /əʊ/ (*goat*), /aʊ/ (*mouth*) and /aɪ/ (*price*). In the majority of UK accents, these dipthongs include a lot of tongue and lip movement, but in MLE the vowel is reduced to a monopthong, where there is less articulatory movement. This means that a word such as *face* sounds more like 'fes' than Received Pronunciation 'fays' or Cockney 'fayis'.

- A more syllable-timed rhythm, meaning that speech takes on a 'staccato' quality, where syllable duration is more regular when compared with non-MLE, stress-timed accents.

- A change in the way that definite and indefinite articles are used. /ðə/ rather than /ðiː/ is used for 'the', and 'a' /ə/ is used instead of 'an' /ən/ before words that begin with a vowel, such as *a apple* rather than *an apple*.

- In terms of vocabulary, lexical innovations tend to be in the form of borrowings from Jamaican English. This is a neat example of the Founder Principle, where the lexicon of an area's founding population continues to survive despite the arrival of later, different, immigrant groups.

Processes of language change

Words borrowed in this way include *blood* and *bredren* ('friend'), *ends* ('neighbourhood') and *whagwan* ('what's up').

- Lower frequency of h-dropping than in other London dialects.

ACTIVITY 3.3
Your own sociophonetic profile

In this activity, you will be creating and reflecting on your own sociophonetic profile. It may be useful to use a sound recorder (available for free on most mobile phones and computers) to help you compile a database of speech recordings. The phonetic analysis software *Praat* is also a useful tool for recording and analysing spoken language, and is available to download for free at: www.cambridge.org/links/esccha6003.

1. Record yourself saying the words *face*, *goat*, *mouth* and *price*. Put them into a sentence so you can obtain as natural sounding a recording as possible. Transcribe the sentences using the phonetic alphabet (see the IPA chart on page 110) and analyse the vowels. Are they the prototypical diphthongs of /eɪ/, /əʊ/, /aʊ/ and /aɪ/, or are they variations of these?

2. Record yourself saying the sentences *I'm going for a bath* and *we're going up there*. Focus on the vowel in *bath* and *up*. Do you use a long /a:/ or a short /æ/ for *bath*, or a /ʌ/ or a /ʊ/ for *up*?

3. Compare your findings with somebody else's. If there are differences, can you account for them in terms of your sociolinguistic backgrounds? You could also explore the Sounds Familiar? page on the British Library's website, a database of spoken language recordings representing different accents and dialects of the UK: www.cambridge.org/links/esccha6004.

4. Now record a two-minute natural conversation with somebody else. Transcribe the conversation and focus on the use of th-fronting. To what extent do you do this?

3.5 Grammatical change

This section explores how the grammar of English has changed over time. This tends to be a slower process of language change when compared to lexical and semantic change.

3 Language change

Chapter 2 looked at some of the major changes in the English grammatical system over time, such as the loss of case, changes in pronouns and the gradual rigidity in word order. As a descendent from Germanic languages, English began as a language that made extensive use of inflectional morphology to signal grammatical distinctions. However, the arrival of the Vikings and their linguistic influence meant that this system collapsed. This shift was one of the biggest changes in the history of English grammar.

The rest of this section looks at some of the attitudes towards grammatical change. Chapter 5 will cover attitudes in more detail. Grammar changes much more slowly than words or meanings, and newer changes can often be the source of anger and frustration for many – especially older, more conservative speakers. The Queen's English Society (QES) is a perfect example of such a group, which states in its constitution that its aim is to:

> promote the maintenance, knowledge, understanding, development and appreciation of the English language as used both in speech and writing; to educate the public in its correct and elegant usage; and to discourage the intrusion of anything detrimental to clarity or euphony.

But what exactly is 'correct and elegant usage'? The QES fails to provide a satisfactory explanation, and also fails to acknowledge the importance of linguistic variation and the way that language changes according to context. It does, however, provide what it deems to be a 'useful guide to English' on its website which includes guidance on the 'correct' usage of a range of 'grammatical gripes'. It may surprise you that these were written in the twenty-first century. Three of the QES's objections are dealt with in a linguistically informed way in Table 3.1, taking a critical perspective to the prescription and regulation of language use.

Table 3.1: QES 'guide to English' and some critical responses

Queen's English Society 'guide to English'	A critical reply
Double negatives such as *I don't want no lessons from you* and *he didn't say nothing* are regarded as an illogical 'error'. An analogy to mathematics is made here, where two negatives create a positive, so that *he didn't say nothing* means *he said something*.	• Language is not maths, and so the analogy does not work here. • Many regional varieties of English (such as Lancashire and Yorkshire) use double, and even triple, negatives. They are an important marker of linguistic identity.

Processes of language change

Queen's English Society 'guide to English'	A critical reply
	• In actual communication, double negatives are never interpreted as the positive meaning of an expression, and do not yield a communication breakdown. • Many languages (including Spanish, Portuguese and French, where we 'borrowed' many words from) use double negatives. • Many writers (including Chaucer and Shakespeare) make extensive use of double negatives.
Personal pronouns should be in the 'correct form and order' – such as *my husband and I* and not *me and my husband*. In the second example, *me* is functioning as the Subject, but English grammar only allows it to function as the Object, as in the first – correct – example.	• In polite and formal contexts it may well be appropriate to use *my husband and I*. But not all situations of language use are polite and formal contexts. • Shifting the *me* to the front of the clause can have a desired stylistic effect of emphasis, especially if used with stress or an increase in volume. • This is a 'politeness rule' rather than a 'grammatical rule'.
Verbless sentences are constructions that should 'never be used in formal writing or by schoolchildren in their work'. Established writers are 'allowed to commit occasional grammatical errors', but if they use verbless sentences, then they 'do so at their own risk'.	• Writing a sentence without a verb can be a powerful and stylistically appropriate choice of language in the right context. • For example, consider the opening to *Bleak House* by Charles Dickens, who creates a striking image of Victorian London without using a single finite verb:

3 Language change

Queen's English Society 'guide to English'	A critical reply
	Fog on the Essex marshes, fog on the Kentish heights. Fog creeping into the cabooses of collier-brigs; fog lying out on the yards, and hovering in the rigging of great ships; fog drooping on the gunwales of barges and small boats. Fog in the eyes and throats of ancient Greenwich pensioners, wheezing by the firesides of their wards; fog in the stem and bowl of the afternoon pipe of the wrathful skipper, down in his close cabin; fog cruelly pinching the toes and fingers of his shivering little 'prentice boy on deck.
	• Language is a resource from which we can make choices. To state that a construction should 'never' be used is denying the right of people to access the resources of a language.

Hopefully what has become clear in this criticism is that:

- It makes no sense to talk about the 'correct' use of a language without the consideration of context. This is not to say that 'anything goes', but that we adapt and shape our language according to the sociocultural situation of use.
- English is not an 'object' to be defended or owned. The very name of the QES implies that this metaphor underpins the work of the group. Nobody has privileged rights to use or prescribe English, in the way that the QES appear to position itself.
- The LANGUAGE IS AN OBJECT TO BE DEFENDED metaphor has dangerous implications for the promotion of nationalism and jingoism.
- Grammar is a RESOURCE, not a RULEBOOK.
- 'Helpful' guides such as those published by the QES are not in fact helpful, but can be damaging and dangerous in promoting a form of linguistic imperialism, which is explored further in Chapter 5.
- Those who love the study of language do so because of variation and change: it's what makes linguistics interesting.

Processes of language change

3.5.1 Morphological change

Morphology is defined as the internal structure of words. It has two main subdivisions: inflection and derivation.

Inflection is concerned with how word structure is affected by other words in sentences. For example, a pronoun like *she* can take the forms *she*, *her* and *hers* depending on whether it is functioning as the Subject, Object or a possessive. Verbs *inflect* when they exhibit different tenses: *walk, walking* and *walked*.

Derivation is where new words are created, either with new meanings (for example, *malnourish* is derived from *nourish*) or with new grammatical properties (for example, we can form adverbs by using the base adjective, as in *slowly* derived from *slow*). Section 3.2.2 provided some more examples of this.

As well as these processes, there are various other types of morphological change. Two of them are explored below.

- **Reanalysis** is where a word contains two separate roots that have coalesced into a compound, meaning that the new word has to be 'reanalysed' as a whole. For example, *hair* (noun) + *cut* (verb) created the compound noun *haircut*.

- **Analogy** is where new words simply adopt the morphological patterns that already exist in the language. For example, when speakers introduced the noun *Brexiteer* into English, they did so by applying existing morphological patterns – in this case, adding the *–eer* suffix to *Brexit*, which is used to denote a person or a thing that does something. Young children are able to do this very easily when they are shown new words, such as in Jean Berko's famous *wug test*, where children were able to apply the plural marker *–s* onto the noun *wug*. As humans, we tend to prefer regular patterns over irregular patterns, and so there is a cognitive basis for analogical processes of morphological change. Of course, analogies are often so embedded into the structure of a language that they become a grammatical rule of word formation. This is one reason why irregular nouns and verbs look odd and can be difficult for non-native speakers or young children – such as *octopi* and the past tense of *swim* (*swam*, not *swimmed*).

3.6 What causes change?

In this chapter, you have seen that speakers of a language are highly innovative and creative when it comes to developing and changing language. Many new forms are a result of sociocultural changes such as technology, exploration and language contact, with English speakers seeing other languages as a 'resource

3 Language change

pool' from which words can be taken and adapted. There are hundreds of reasons for language change, and whilst there are too many to cover them all here, the more widely researched reasons are outlined below.

3.6.1 Variation and prestige

Change is sometimes a result of certain linguistic forms having perceived prestige over others. Certain individuals or speech communities might be 'linguistically attractive' and become seen as fashionable. Accommodation theory argues that speakers tend to *converge* (become more linguistically similar) towards others when they wish to reduce social distance and create a sense of a speech community. They tend to *diverge* (become less linguistically similar) when they wish to emphasise their distinctiveness or idiosyncrasies.

> **KEY TERM**
>
> **Accommodation theory:** a sociolinguistic theory arguing that speakers modify their speaking style to become more like or less like the people they are speaking to

3.6.2 Language contact and superdiversity

We live in an increasingly globalised world, with more and more people living in densely populated urban areas than ever before. This means that languages and dialects come into regular contact with each other – this, of course, is nothing new for English as it has always been a highly 'sociable' language. There is now a large body of research and a growing interest in the way that Englishes are used around the world, bringing about exciting and innovative changes in the language. This is explored further in Chapter 5.

3.6.3 Language planning

Most changes to a language occur naturally, but sometimes change is the result of deliberate external intervention. This is known as language planning. Decisions about how language should be used are made every day – from small-scale, local interventions such as the banning of particular slang forms in schools, to large-scale, global interventions such as a government deciding to adopt or change its official language. It is typically those that hold authority that impose language planning, and there are always political and ideological motivations behind decisions. Ironically, language planning is rarely about language, but more about social, political and economic factors. English has undergone various forms of language planning, such as the publication of

Samuel Johnson's 1755 dictionary, which sought to standardise spelling and meaning. And UK National Curriculum documents for schools are a form of language planning, decreeing that all children become familiar with the uses and purposes of Standard English.

3.6.4 Inter-generational change and language acquisition

If you speak to somebody from a much older or younger generation than you, then you will no doubt notice that they use language in a variety of different ways to you. Indeed, differences in language use across generations are one of the more immediately obvious pieces of evidence that language is changing. Every generation makes its own contribution to language change, and when enough time has passed, these differences become increasingly noticeable. Generations differ in the way they use language because they were brought up in different sociocultural environments, and so are likely to have views about the world that reflect this. This can be manifested in lexical, semantic, grammatical and phonological differences, but also in different attitudes and perceptions towards language use. The next chapter explores these kinds of things further.

RESEARCH QUESTION
Comparing texts over time

Find two texts from different eras of English that are from the same genre. For example, you could compare an extract from a recipe book, novel or religious text from Middle English with one from Present Day English. Using what you have learnt about the processes of language change in this chapter, compare the texts in the way that they use language.

- Explore the etymological roots of a selection of words from both texts.
- Compare the lexical and grammatical style. Is one text more formal than the other, for example? How do you know?
- Have any words undergone a semantic shift? If so, what kind?
- Use Google Ngram Viewer to investigate and compare particular words or phrases from both texts.
- Think about the sociocultural contexts of each text and how this might have shaped the way language is used.

Language change

Wider reading

You can find out more about the topics in this chapter by reading the following:

Lexical change and semantic change

McWhorter, J. (2016). *Words on the Move: Why English Won't – and Can't – Sit Still (Like, Literally)*. New York: Henry Holt and Company.

Trask, R.L. (1996). *Historical Linguistics*. London: Routledge.

Phonological change

Cruttenden, A. (2008). *Gimson's Pronunciation of English*. London: Routledge.

Honeybone, P. (2012). 'Lenition in English'. In Nevalainen, T. & Traugott, E. (eds). *The Oxford Handbook of the History of English*. Oxford: Oxford University Press.

Grammatical change

Hollmann, W. (2009). 'Grammatical change'. In J. Culpeper, F. Katamba, P. Kerswill & T. McEnery (eds). *English Language: Description, Variation and Context*. Basingstoke: Palgrave, pp 314–333.

Reasons for change

Holmes, J. & Wilson, N. (2017). *An Introduction to Sociolinguistics* (Fifth edition). London: Routledge.

Wright, S. (2016). *Language Policy and Language Planning: From Nationalism to Globalisation* (Second edition). Basingstoke: Palgrave.

Chapter 4
Attitudes to language change

In this chapter, you will:

- Explore some of the different attitudes to language usage, variation and change
- Consider why different attitudes exist and what factors drive them
- Critically analyse texts that project different attitudes to language usage, variation and change

4 Language change

4.1 Language, politics and ideologies

Attitudes to language usage, variation and change are rarely, if ever, just about language. Language is political, and there are often agendas and ideologies at the heart of the debate. This view of language was taken up by Deborah Cameron, in her 1995 work *Verbal Hygiene*, who argued that people with conservative views:

> use 'grammar' as the metaphorical correlate for a cluster of related political and moral terms: *order, tradition, authority, hierarchy* and *rules*. In the ideological world that conservatives inhabit, these terms are not only positive, they define the conditions for any civil society, while their opposites – *disorder, change, fragmentation, anarchy* and *lawlessness* – signify the breakdown of social relations. A panic about grammar is therefore interpretable as the metaphorical expression of persistent conservative fears that we are losing the values that underpin civilization and sliding into chaos. (Cameron 1995: 96)

In other words, using 'bad grammar' can mean 'behaving badly'. And because 'bad grammar' is so often aligned with new forms of a language that arise as a result of grammatical change, we can understand this attitude in terms of metaphor:

CONFORMING TO GRAMMATICAL RULES IS CONFORMING TO SOCIETY

CONFORMING TO GRAMMATICAL RULES IS A STATEMENT OF AUTHORITY

RESISTING LANGUAGE CHANGE IS GOOD BEHAVIOUR

As you will see in this chapter, this view of language is conservative and prescriptive. It supposes that there is a 'correct' way to use English, and that any changes to a language – especially those that challenge the standard variety – are damaging and threaten the very identity of 'proper English'. This is especially relevant in a globalised world, where English is increasingly used in ways that deviate from the standard. Because many people believe that English 'belongs' to Britain, they see it as their right and their role to defend changes and deviations. But – as you have seen throughout this book – language always changes. So isn't trying to defend something as slippery and dynamic as language a rather futile task?

Given the idea that attitudes to language change are inherently political, a useful approach to studying language can be found in Critical Discourse Analysis (CDA), such as the work by Norman Fairclough in his 2014 book *Language and Power*. CDA is attractive because it acknowledges the ways that language is often a projection of political and ideological views. Chapter 4 of *Attitudes to Language* (in this series) by Dan Clayton explores this method in more detail. In short, people who have prescriptive, conservative views to language often hold traditional, nationalist and parochial views on society itself.

Attitudes to language change

> **KEY TERM**
> **Critical Discourse Analysis:** an approach to the study of both written and spoken language focusing on the ways that power is enacted

4.2 Prescription and description

The distinction between prescriptive and descriptive approaches to grammar is an important one in linguistics. Prescriptivists can be thought of as people who want to tell us how we *ought* to use language, while descriptivists want to tell us how we actually *do* use language. Rather than being a clear-cut, oppositional distinction, prescriptive and descriptive attitudes are best thought of as existing along a scale. The research task at the end of this chapter asks you to think about this further.

It should be noted that in certain contexts, all people probably hold some prescriptivist values. For example, a linguist who self-identifies as a descriptive liberal is still practising a form of prescriptivism if she asks her students to write an essay in a certain way, or objects to the way that a certain word is used, if it conflicts with her own ideas. This chapter will ask you to think about your own values and attitudes to language change.

Prescriptive and descriptive attitudes are manifested in different ways – one of them being 'grammars' of a language. Grammars are (usually) comprehensive handbooks, detailing the structure of a language. The following sections look at prescriptive and descriptive grammars in more detail.

4.2.1 Prescription

Prescriptive grammars can be thought of as usage manuals – they are typically arranged like a dictionary, containing an alphabetically sorted list of grammar topics that essentially tell their readers the 'correct' way to use language. The 'correct' version of English, according to prescriptive grammars, is Standard English, meaning that prescriptive grammars will often confuse informality with ungrammaticality. Section 4.3 argues for a reframing of 'correctness' to 'appropriateness', suggesting the term register as a useful notion here.

Prescriptive grammars also tend to be selective in what they cover, focusing on common 'errors' rather than the actual details of a language. Huddleston and Pullum (2002: 7) label this as 'aesthetic authoritarianism', where views on language usage and change are driven by no more than the author's personal

4 Language change

tastes. This does *not* mean that acquiring knowledge of Standard English is not a desirable skill: it is highly desirable, but only if users understand that it exists alongside other variations of English, and that usage of any variety depends on the sociocultural context of usage.

> **KEY TERM**
>
> **Register:** a particular variety of language as defined according to the way it is used in social situations and different contexts – for example, a register of formal English; a register of business English, etc.

Text 4A is the opening to *Eats, Shoots and Leaves* by Lynne Truss (2003), a widely sold 'zero-tolerance' usage guide to grammar, punctuation and spelling. It provides a good example of the views held by prescriptivists.

Text 4A

> Either this will ring bells for you, or it won't. A printed banner has appeared on the concourse of a petrol station near to where I live. 'Come inside,' it says, 'for CD's, VIDEO's, DVD's, and BOOK's.'
>
> If this satanic sprinkling of redundant apostrophes causes no little gasp of horror or quickening of the pulse, you should probably put down this book at once. By all means congratulate yourself that you are not a pedant or even a stickler; that you are happily equipped to live in a world of plummeting punctuation standards; but just don't bother to go any further. For any true stickler, you see, the sight of the plural word 'Book's' with an apostrophe in it will trigger a ghastly private emotional process similar to the stages of bereavement, though greatly accelerated. First there is shock. Within seconds, shock gives way to disbelief, disbelief to pain, and pain to anger. Finally (and this is where the analogy breaks down), anger gives way to a righteous urge to perpetrate an act of criminal damage with the aid of a permanent marker.

Truss clearly feels strongly about language. She equates feelings caused by language use to the death of a loved one, and evokes images of the devil to describe people who use certain linguistic forms. Although her writing may appear humorous, there are some serious issues with these kinds of attitudes. Firstly, Truss's argument is flawed. She seems to base her views on the imaginary idea that at some point in the past there was a 'golden age' of grammar, when everybody was capable of using 'correct' forms of English, and that those abilities

Attitudes to language change

have gradually declined over time. This is called a declinist view of language change, an ideological view criticised by Lane Greene (2011: 47):

> A hundred and forty years ago, one in five Americans was illiterate. Now less than one in a hundred is – and this fall began during a hundred years of 'separate but equal' dismal schools for blacks in America. In Britain, illiteracy is rarer still. It may be true that formal grammar was taught more extensively in good schools in the past. But the notion that once upon a time, every schoolboy was an H.W. Fowler, every schoolgirl a perfectly punctuating Lynne Truss, but today no one can put two words together simply holds no water. Where is the former golden age of the written word?

KEY TERM
Declinist/declinism: a tendency noted by Lane Greene for prescriptivists to view language as being in a state of constant decline from a once great peak

This 'golden age' never existed. And yet, every generation and every era of language change has a body of people who pine for it, who yearn nostalgically for an (imaginary) time where people spoke 'properly' and 'falling standards' were tackled head on. One of the earliest and most publicised complaints about the English language came from Jonathan Swift, who, in his 1712 public letter entitled *A Proposal for Correcting, Improving and Ascertaining the English Tongue*, wrote:

> our Language is extremely imperfect; that its daily Improvements are by no means in proportion to its daily Corruptions; and the Pretenders to polish and refine it, have chiefly multiplied Abuses and Absurdities; and, that in many Instances, it offends against every Part of Grammar.

Swift's idea was to create an academy for the protection and defence of the English language, much like French prescriptivists had done in the shape of the *Académie Française*. He proposed that:

> some Method should be thought on for ascertaining and fixing our Language for ever, after such Alterations are made in it as shall be thought requisite.

Modern-day prescriptivists continue to yearn and pine for this imaginary golden age of language. And they are not hard to find: looming large in the pages of the (mostly right-wing) media, and in bestseller usage guides such as those by Lynne Truss (2003), John Humphrys (2005) and Nevile Gwynne (2013). Section 4.2.3

4 Language change

explores some of the reasons why the voice of prescriptivism continues to be heard. Indeed, the very fact that prescriptivism prevails is a fascinating area of language study. To dismiss or brush off the prescriptivists would be counter to the aims of descriptive linguistics, which are to describe and understand all forms of language and discourse *about* language.

Case study: prescriptivism in action

In April 2017, a news story about a Bristolian self-styled 'grammar vigilante' came about, concerning a man who spends his nights covertly correcting misplaced or missing apostrophes on shop signs, posters and billboards. Is this prescriptivism, or is it just innocuous fun? Before you read on, you might like to think about your own ideas on this issue.

An article by the linguist Rob Drummond (2017) argued that such behaviour normalises and champions prescriptivism, and only serves to promote the idea that it's acceptable to pick on people because of the way they use language. Despite the fact that the rules for when the apostrophe should and shouldn't be used are not as fixed as you might think, prescriptivists are often quick to point out – and laugh at – other people's linguistic choices. Apostrophe mis/usage might seem like a minor 'offence', but if these kinds of attitudes are scaled up to things such as accents, dialects and entire languages then it quickly becomes a much more serious issue. To make the point clear: is there any difference between deriding someone for misplacing an apostrophe and deriding someone for choosing to speak in a local dialect? What about the difference between deriding someone for misplacing an apostrophe and deriding someone who chooses to speak in their native language rather than English? Although the 'gap' between these things might appear large, the underlying values, ideologies and attitudes towards language are similar.

4.2.2 Description

Descriptive grammars resemble a documentary, in that they describe and document the way that language is used, varies and changes. They do not deride or bemoan change, but acknowledge it as an interesting aspect of language. Instead of complaining about a new word or pronunciation (as in the prescriptivist tradition), descriptive linguists seek to collect linguistic data with the aim of exploring and understanding patterns. This is a serious undertaking, and the well-known comprehensive grammars of the English language are thousands of pages long. They are also never 'complete', considering the fact that language undergoes a constant process of change. As such, descriptive grammars provide a synchronic snapshot of what a language looks like at a particular moment in time.

4.2.3 Why do prescriptivism and descriptivism exist?

You might think that prescriptive grammars are rather outdated. All linguists would certainly agree that they have no place in modern linguistics, and clash with the aims of the discipline. And yet, they continue to be published, bought and revered. Prescriptivism is very much alive and well. Consult the comments section of any online article about language use and change, and you will find a breeding ground for prescriptive views on language. But why does prescriptivism continue? Where do prescriptive attitudes come from? The answers lie with something that was covered at the very beginning of this chapter: attitudes to language are always about more than *just* language. Some of the reasons why attitudes to language exist include the following:

- The general public tends not to question the need for prescriptivism, and instead it becomes seen as common sense. To many people, the need for grammar rules is as common sense as the rules themselves. Cameron argues that 'the idea that some ways of speaking and writing may be preferred to others, that linguistic performance may legitimately be evaluated and if necessary criticized, is absolutely central to the ordinary speaker's whole conception of language' (1997: 10).

- The media often consult non-linguists about real-world language issues, or include very limited comments from linguists. For example, a *Daily Telegraph* story about the lack of punctuation marks on the new £5 note in England featured just one short statement from a linguist and multiple statements from non-linguists. This meant that the angle of the story was biased in favour of prescriptive views, downplaying the voice and opinions of descriptive linguists. Sadly, many articles about language follow a similar pattern. In turn, the public gets limited exposure and education about language from the perspective of linguists.

- The media often misrepresent linguistic research so it becomes reframed as prescriptivism, rather than the descriptive work found in the original research. See the case on vocal fry, in Section 4.4.1 of this chapter, for an example of this.

- Language is an integral part of identity and perceived behaviour. So-called 'etiquette guides' have always been popular, and give advice about dress codes and table manners alongside language use. Michael Halliday labels this kind of prescription as 'linguistic table-manners' (2009: 431), promoting artificial rules that can gradually become part of a speaker's repertoire.

- People's beliefs about language are grounded in a lifetime of usage: established in childhood and built up through experience. Thus, people tend to be rather sensitive and nostalgic about language, often becoming set

4 Language change

in their ways, and see change as an intrusive threat to their linguistic and personal identity.

- There is a belief that prescriptivism is necessary for efficacy, clarity and language maintenance, as well as supporting ideologies around nationalism and linguistic imperialism.

- Standard English is seen as the norm in schools, often at the expense of other varieties. Activity 4.1 explores attitudes to language usage, variation and change in the context of education in further detail.

4.2.4 Register

The notion of register is an important and useful one when it comes to describing linguistic usage, variation and change. This rejects the contrast between 'correct' and 'incorrect' language, reframing language as 'a series of contextually appropriate choices'. To be clear: this does not mean that descriptive linguists think that 'anything goes' in language.

ACTIVITY 4.1
Register and re-writing

Read Text 4B, a reproduction of a sign placed on the gates of a school in south London in 2013.

Despite its obvious prescriptive attitudes, this sign raises an important point about language, in that certain linguistic choices are more appropriate than others, in certain contexts. Write a text that adopts a more descriptive approach to this issue, suitable for young children. For example, you could:

- Create a lesson plan for primary school children where they learn about different attitudes to language.

- Write an extract from a National Curriculum document providing guidance and information about what aspects and attitudes to language should be studied in schools.

- Rewrite Text 4B so that it acknowledges the importance of *register* and *appropriateness*, rather than framing language in terms of *correctness*.

You should consider what is meant by *register* in your writing. Once your text is complete, provide a short commentary on your own writing, where you reflect and justify the choices you made. See Giovanelli (2016) for an interesting discussion of language policing in schools.

Attitudes to language change

Text 4B

> **Banned Words:**
>
> COZ   AINT
>
> LIKE   BARE
>
> EXTRA   INNIT
>
> YOU WOZ and WE WOZ
>
> Beginning sentences with BASICALLY
>
> Ending sentences with YEAH

4.3 Metaphors and attitudes to change

Text 4C is an extract from an article published in *The Telegraph* in October 2006. It was written by John Humphrys, a well known prescriptivist and author of various 'pop-linguistic' books such as *Lost for Words: The Mangling and Manipulating of the English Language*. As you read Text 4C, think about the metaphors that underpin Humphrys' views of what language is, and his attitude to language change. *Today* is a radio programme co-presented by Humphrys.

Text 4C

Mind your language – it matters!

'Understanding the basic workings of grammar liberates. If you don't know how to construct a sentence, how can you express yourself?'

In the first exclusive extract from his new book on language, Humphrys argues that we must safeguard grammar and clarity in an age of texting, slang and hype.

There are one or two certainties on Today. You know that a story about cruelty to animals will always get a bigger reaction than one about cruelty to children. You know particular subjects will stir great passion in the breasts of a certain section of Radio 4 listeners: 'elf 'n' safety rules; political correctness gone mad; anything about the Union Jack and, of course, anything about the English language. It is one thing we have in common. All of us. You and I and the slightly menacing young hoodie hanging around on the street corner. We all care about language. Your concern may be different from the young hoodie's.

4 Language change

> You might contemplate climbing Everest naked before splitting an infinitive. He cares just as passionately about using language that proves his street cred. We each need to take care. His language is changing almost every day. A word that was a compliment yesterday may be an insult tomorrow. Ours is changing too – more slowly, but just as surely.
>
> Language is more than a tool for expressing ourselves. It acts as a mirror to our world, reflecting back to us the way we live. It reflects our attitudes about the way we see things and how we are seen by others: in public life; in politics and commerce; in advertising and marketing; in broadcasting and journalism. Yet the prevailing wisdom about language seems to be that 'anything goes'. Word by word, we are at risk of dragging our language down to the lowest common denominator and we do so at the cost of its most precious qualities: subtlety and precision. If we're happy to let our common public language be used in this way, communication will be reduced to a narrow range of basic meanings.

Linguists would no doubt agree with certain things that Humphrys touches on, namely, the idea that language *does* matter. Nobody would disagree with the sentiment here – linguist or not. But Humphrys' prescriptive views are soon made obvious when you think about the way that he construes what language is, and *what* it matters for. Metaphor is a particularly useful tool for exploring attitudes, perceptions and ideologies that people hold, and you can find the following metaphors in the text:

BEING LITERATE IS FREEDOM
'Understanding the basic workings of grammar liberates'

PARTS OF A LANGUAGE ARE CONSTRUCTION MATERIALS
'If you don't know how to construct a sentence'

GRAMMAR IS AN OBJECT TO BE DEFENDED
'We must safeguard grammar'
'We do so at the cost of its precious qualities'

USING 'INCORRECT' GRAMMAR IS A DANGEROUS ACTIVITY
'You might contemplate climbing Everest naked before splitting an infinitive'

DOWN/SMALL IS BAD
'We are at risk of dragging our language down to the lowest common denominator'

'Communication will be reduced to a narrow range of basic meanings'

Attitudes to language change

The 'anything goes' argument that Humphrys invokes is a popular one amongst prescriptivists. And yet, it is not a view that descriptive linguists hold. Instead, descriptive linguists argue that language use is contextually bound, and that context yields different levels of appropriateness. Once again, the importance of register is apparent as a useful way of describing usage, variation and change.

4.3.1 Aitchison's metaphors

In a 1996 lecture entitled *A Web of Worries*, Jean Aitchison questioned the way that language change was represented in the media, citing examples such as 'we are plagued with idiots on radio and television who speak English like the dregs of humanity, to the detriment of our children' and 'the language the world is crying out to learn is diseased in its own country'. Aitchison argued that such views of language change were evidence of people being ill-informed on linguistic matters, and that such views are somewhat futile, given the inevitability of change. For her, many people's ideas on language were outdated – a 'cobweb of old ideas [that] ensnares people as they think about language'.

Although she didn't use the X IS Y convention for structuring metaphors, she argued that most journalism drew on three assumptions to represent people's attitudes to language change, which can be re-written as the following metaphors:

1   LANGUAGE CHANGE IS A DISEASE

2   LANGUAGE CHANGE IS LAZY BEHAVIOUR

3   LANGUAGE IS A LISTED BUILDING

The first metaphor, LANGUAGE CHANGE IS A DISEASE, is often called the 'infectious disease' assumption. This is based on the idea that we somehow 'catch' changes from each other, and that we ought to fight and resist these changes. You might notice that this resonates with a metaphor picked out from Cameron's work, namely one of RESISTING LANGUAGE CHANGE IS GOOD BEHAVIOUR. Aitchison acknowledges the fact that change comes about because of social contact, as do diseases – but that things catch on and people change because *they want to*: they want to adhere to social groups, follow the latest trends, and so on. The DISEASE metaphor also rests on the assumption that there is some kind of 'cure' or 'vaccine' for successfully treating language change. If change is a disease, then are prescriptivists and groups such as the Queen's English Society the doctors? If so, the disease is winning.

The second metaphor, LANGUAGE CHANGE IS LAZY BEHAVIOUR is often called the 'damp spoon' assumption. This is based on the idea that certain forms of language are 'vulgar' and 'lazy': the reaction that some people might have when somebody leaves a damp spoon in the sugar bowl, or spreads butter with the bread knife. This view assumes that it is sloppiness and laziness that

4 Language change

causes languages to change – the idea that people simply cannot be bothered to articulate speech sounds or write 'properly'. As you saw in Chapter 3, processes of phonological change mean that speakers do indeed change the articulation of speech sounds, but this is not because of laziness – it's because of muscular efficiency and various types of connected speech phenomena.

The third and final metaphor, LANGUAGE IS A LISTED BUILDING, is often called the 'crumbling castle' assumption, and is underpinned by a declinist view. This is based on the idea that the English language is a beautiful, old building that needs to be protected and preserved. Aitchison criticises the way people often treat language, as if it were like 'parks, national forests, monuments, and public utilities […] available for properly respectful use but not for defacement or destruction'. She goes on to say that the metaphor itself simply doesn't hold, because it implies the language was once carefully and lovingly constructed, until it reached a point of maximum aesthetic splendour. Note that this idea resonates with the fictional 'golden age' of grammar that prescriptivists often yearn for, something that was covered in Section 4.2.1.

LANGUAGE IS A TIDAL FLOW

To try and resist such metaphors, in 1999 the linguist David Crystal proposed the metaphor of LANGUAGE IS A TIDAL FLOW to explain language change. This metaphor captures the idea that language is like a tide – constantly changing and shifting in unpredictable ways, whilst retaining some form of uniformity and pattern. The tide brings in new words and removes others in natural ways. In adopting this metaphor, Crystal argues that a view of language change shifts towards one where changes are not for the worse or better, but 'just changes, sometimes going one way, sometimes another' (1999: 2).

4.4 Attitudes to phonological change

This section considers some of the attitudes around certain types of phonological change – that is, the way that people sound when they speak.

4.4.1 Vocal fry

If you articulate a vowel sound slowly, tense your vocal folds and don't allow much air to pass through them, then you may well be producing a sound known as vocal fry or creaky voice. This feature of pronunciation was the subject of much media attention in 2011, when *Science Now* reported that:

> A curious vocal pattern has crept into the speech of young adult women who speak American English: low, creaky vibrations, also called vocal fry. Pop singers, such as Britney Spears, slip vocal fry into their music as a way

Attitudes to language change

to reach low notes and add style. Now, a new study of young women in New York State shows that the same guttural vibration – once considered a speech disorder – has become a language fad.

> **KEY TERM**
> **Vocal fry/creaky voice:** a way of speaking that constricts the vocal folds and creates a creaking, low frequency sound

The attention came because an academic journal paper (Wolk, Abdelli-Beruh and Slavin, 2012) had found that vocal fry was a popular form of speech amongst young American women. But the media stories that surrounded it focused on the idea that this was somehow a new form, propelled into mainstream usage by celebrities such as Britney Spears and Kim Kardashian. In fact, it has been around for a much longer time, as highlighted in a blog post on the *Language Log*: (www.cambridge.org/links/esccha6010). Deficit views of vocal fry soon emerged in the UK media, with these 'destructive speech patterns' (www.cambridge.org/links/esccha6011) being blamed on hurting women's job prospects – despite the fact that it is also a phonological feature of men's speech. Again, we see an example of prescriptive attitudes to change tied up with wider discourses around gender, age and status – all of which is based on the misreporting of academic research. Text 4D is a selection of tweets expressing various attitudes to vocal fry.

Text 4D

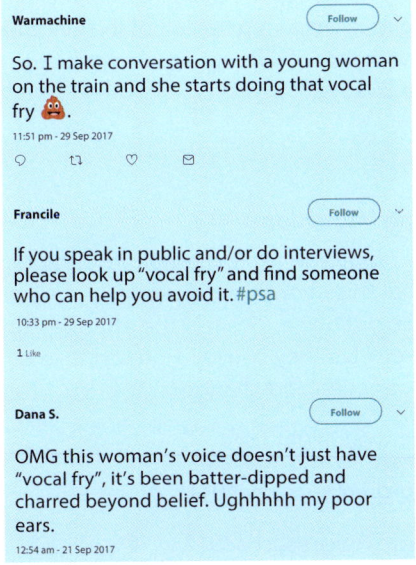

4 Language change

4.4.2 Rising intonation

Rising intonation is a phonological feature that has attracted much attention in the press, the general public and in linguistic research. Normally an intonation pattern heard at the end of questions, rising intonation is increasingly used with statements, especially over the last 20–30 years. Despite a widespread discourse in the media that uptalk displays uncertainty and insecurity, the linguist Paul Warren (2015) argues that rising intonation actually has a wide range of social and semantic functions. For example, it is often used when the speaker is the owner of the information rather than the seeker of information, and is used as an invitation to communicate, rather than simply checking understanding or showing insecurity.

> **KEY TERM**
>
> **Rising intonation:** using a rising tone as an utterance ends. Generally used when asking a question, but now more prevalent in statements. Can also be referred to as high-rising terminals or uptalk

Warren criticises the way that certain social groups – particularly young women – have been lambasted in the press and the public. He argues that the link between uptalk and young women is based on stereotypes, not linguistic research. And the results of his research conclude that:

> We have seen that uptalk is not exclusively linked to young speakers, nor to women. Increasingly it is reported in the speech of older speakers, and in that of men. It would perhaps be more appropriate to consider uptalk's distribution among speakers as a reflection of the functions that it fulfils and of the needs or desires of different speaker groups to express those functions. (Warren 2015: 189)

> **ACTIVITY 4.2**
>
> **Attitudes to rising intonation**
>
> Search online for 'uptalk' or 'rising intonation' and prepare a report about the ways that this phonological property is represented in the press and in public discourse. How do the attitudes compare with the work of Paul Warren? Do they convey a prescriptive or descriptive view of language use, variation and change?
>
> As a starting point, you might try:
>
> www.cambridge.org/links/esccha6011
>
> www.cambridge.org/links/esccha6012

4.5 Attitudes to lexical change

In Chapter 3, some of the processes of lexical change were explored. In the following sections, some of the attitudes towards this type of change are presented.

4.5.1 Americanisms

British English speakers have long held attitudes towards the American influence on English. For some people, Americanisms are a 'corruptive force' that are 'killing' the English language, as suggested in a 2017 book by Matthew Engel. In the book, Engel rallies British English speakers to 'defend' the English language, seemingly misunderstanding that language is *not* a physical object that can be owned and protected and that the metaphor of LANGUAGE IS WAR is an inappropriate way to think about language change. But, Engel is not alone in such prescriptive views. A quick look at the *Cambridge English Corpus* reveals some interesting attitudes, as shown in Figure 4.1.

Figure 4.1: Cambridge English Corpus results for *Americanisms*

more than somewhat.) Readers are probably more accustomed to **Americanisms** or even Britishisms but the change was pleasant. There was no appreciabl
I trust they will follow this dictat up by purging the airwaves of all **Americanisms** . Like gotten, whatever, totally, that rocks, and I nec
they had met. They wondered at his pure German, the absence of **Americanisms** , his love for the language. One wrote: "You spoke about your life without
:17:07am   Isn't it just the way things are heading here? **Americanisms** have crept in to our language cool, like, that's SO awesome! NOT! and our
› <p> RT @[Name812]: Hmm. Emails complaining I use too many **Americanisms** in my columns. I'm so done with that. I'll kick it to the kerb, g … </p><p
are expected to be able to spell correctly when you have so many **Americanisms** shoved in their faces. Let's face it, television is a part of life and if used
around, pat each other on the back, and show little fear. They use **Americanisms** , even though most aren't American. When their children achieve their goa
ill Sullivan a sissy because of his legwear. Like so many **Americanisms** , the name soon made its way across the Atlantic. But if the ter
br a 4-woodfor those of you who are golfers). As for Oz absorbing **Americanisms** , I will respond with the one phrase I bring back. True!" All of th
e things we have been discussing do so because they see them as **Americanisms** or American usages. One such reader wrote, "Recently I saw 'trashed' in a
aile returned to the country of her birth with what she calls all her **Americanisms** in tow. She chronicles her trip in a new book. It's called "Held At A Distanc
en Klinger, Cambridge, Massachussetts Britishisms, like **Americanisms** , are fascinating -at least, they are to me. Charlie has an ancier
 Even in Britain, America's partner in Anglo-Saxon capitalism, **Americanisms** have spread in recent years. The country's most prominent businessman,
n many of the nuances are lost to non-Arabic readers, the off- key **Americanisms** of her own translation are equally revealing. Between syrupy meditations o
oth cap and suspenders socialism." This is yet another example of **Americanisms** creeping into our language but in this case creating a bizarre image at leas
ir isn't wrong to pick up on them. Australians really do use a lot of **Americanisms** , and any novelist who doesn't acknowledge that will be treating Australian
ed an open mind and an infectious enthusiasm. He uses **Americanisms** such as ' and ' to good effect. His speech is la
ednesday ground, they have, for years, been quoting meaningless **Americanisms** , such as "game on". Fortunately, grown men still call each other "love". T
et Margulies's character expressed herself largely through gnomic **Americanisms** . "When you're up to your ass in alligators, it's hard to remember that you
nd. But, unlike Dylan's Guthrie-esque twang and Jagger's tortured **Americanisms** , it's authentic. And if you're susceptible to it, there's a poignan
d you'll see the mediocre talent in "Hell's" is a microcosm of other **Americanisms** , like our If you ran a huge corporation a decade ago, would you F
· Shagged, wuss, enuff, respect, sorted, wicked, geezer and some **Americanisms** - and boy! WOW, yuk, oops, an
» What's over-sexed, over-used and over here in print? **Americanisms** , that's what. Last month Feedback got an e-mail from Malcolm
nd sociological claptrap still flourished, but the infusion of vigorous **Americanisms** and vivid demotic usage from popular culture helped to confound Orwell's
need for plain English. But in a chapter entitled make that titled " **Americanisms** , " the manual betrays both an unseemly nationalistic bias and an ignoran
e 64, Adebayor 78 Arsenal would be wise to learn some **Americanisms** in case Stan Kroenke comes up with a share offer which finds their pukka
afinesque, Medical Flora, I, 158). See also Bart- lett, Dictionary of **Americanisms** , 347, 404. bois de vache, n.m. Buffalo chips. On the Great Plains dried bu
ony: This word and its forms "testify" and "testified" are **Americanisms** we can do without while we have the words "evidence" and "said". <
parts group, and colleagues say he still dots his conversation with **Americanisms** . Most recently he has chaired the trucking group Exel Logistics, which he

Note how many people wish to remove Americanisms from the language, in examples such as 'purging the airwaves of all Americanisms', or the idea of Americanisms 'creeping into' British English. In response to Engel's book, the American linguist Lynne Murphy took a more descriptive, linguistically informed take – Text 4E is an extract from this (you can read the full article here: www.cambridge.org/links/esccha6005).

4 Language change

Text 4E

> Engel has the opinion that Britons should fight against American English. But this opinion is based on various claims or assumptions
>
> - about what English *is* in the US and UK. For example, though he's not southern in origin, the *English* he talks about is very much the south-eastern standard—take, for instance, the claim that *pants* meaning 'trousers' is American and *trousers* is British—a common oversimplification, **but an oversimplification all the same**.
> - about the nature of the 'Britishness' that he wants to protect.
> - about how language changes, and how it is or is not changing in the UK and US. For example, what's the role of regional identity or **social class** in how English changes in Britain?
> - about the relationship between language and culture.
>
> This last point is important. Engel's real enemy is not American words, but changes to British culture. Thatcherism, Blairism, loss of interest in the countryside, all are blamed on 'Americani{s/z}ation'. The extent of that can be debated, but Engel wants to situate the problem in words.

4.5.2 Language change and technology

As discussed in Chapters 2 and 3, technology plays an important role in language change. It brings about new words and meanings, such as *emoji*, *wireless router* and *4G*, and changes the way we actually communicate – with text messages, messenger apps and social media all yielding new and innovative forms.

People's reaction to new technology-related words will often be based on whether they see the technology as having linguistic potential or limitations. People who engage with technology and welcome new inventions are much more likely to have positive reactions to new linguistic forms, whereas people who feel resistant about technology are likely to complain about language change. An interesting illustration of this can be seen by focusing on one particular technological innovation, and examining the attitudes and discourses around this.

The case of emoji

In 2015, *Oxford Dictionaries* named their 'word of the year' as: 😂. Officially known as the 'Face with Tears of Joy' emoji, it was chosen because it was the most frequently used emoji across the entire world that year, made up 20 per cent of all UK emoji use, and reflected a sharp increase in the use of the

Attitudes to language change

word *emoji* itself, indicating a significant shift in the habits of computer-mediated communication. Before reading on, complete Activity 4.3, which asks you about your own attitudes to technology and language change.

> ## KEY TERMS
>
> **Emoji:** a term to describe visual icons (representations of facial expressions, actions and objects) used in social media messaging
>
> **Computer-mediated communication (CMC):** any form of communication that uses the medium of a keyboard or digital device, rather than being spoken or written

ACTIVITY 4.3
Attitudes to technology and change

Oxford Dictionaries' words of the year are selected because of their prevalence in language use (with data taken from language corpora), as well as observations from lexicographers (dictionary editors) and the general public. Table 4.1 lists the words of the year from 2005–2016, from the UK and the USA. Consulting this list, which ones were chosen as a result of technology? What are your reactions to these new forms? Do you use them? If so, in what contexts? What do you think other people's attitudes and reactions to these would have been? If you are unsure about the meaning of any of these words, see if you can work it out before looking them up in a dictionary.

Table 4.1: *Oxford Dictionaries'* words of the year

Year	UK word of the year	USA word of the year
2005	sudoku	podcast
2006	bovvered	carbon-neutral
2007	carbon footprint	locavore
2008	credit crunch	hypermiling
2009	simples	unfriend
2010	big society	refudiate

4 Language change

Year	UK word of the year	USA word of the year
2011	squeezed middle	
2012	omnishambles	GIF (when used as a verb)
2013	selfie	
2014	vape	
2015	😂	
2016	post-truth	

As you might have guessed, complaints about 😂 were commonplace, with most of them questioning the status of 😂 as an actual word. The choice was no doubt brave, but certainly reflected real-life language use and change. Emojis are a particularly interesting example of innovation and change, with Casper Grathwohl, President of Oxford Dictionaries, saying:

> You can see how traditional alphabet scripts have been struggling to meet the rapid-fire, visually focused demands of 21st century communication. It's not surprising that a pictographic script like emoji has stepped in to fill those gaps – it's flexible, immediate, and infuses tone beautifully. As a result, emoji are becoming an increasingly rich form of communication, one that transcends linguistic borders.

This is certainly an extreme-descriptivist view, and did not sit well with many people. Below is a list of comments taken from a *Daily Mail* article about 😂:

a *The degradation of our language continues.*

b *I'm of the generation that can still remember Queen's English. I dread to think which language we'll be speaking in a few years' time.*

c *Simply a crutch for a generation which has such a poor standard of literacy that they have to be given a symbol in order to express their emotions.*

d *Little cartoons for little illiterate (adult) children. This is our future.*

e *I literally don't understand how people survived without emojis. I post at least 10 emojis on every snapchat, Instagram post, Facebook status and Tweet. It's the only way to communicate these days. The vile baby boomers wouldn't understand. They spend their miserable lives complaining about immigrants and watching trash like Coronation Street.*

Attitudes to language change

There are two discourses that emerge from this data:

1. New forms of a language threaten the perceived status of a language, as does the attitude underpinning comment (a). This resonates with Aitchison's ideas on attitudes to language change, perhaps most notably the LANGUAGE IS A LISTED BUILDING metaphor.

2. Different generations have conflicting attitudes towards language change. Although we cannot be certain of the ages of the people who posted the comments above, look again at comments (b), (c), (d) and (e), which all assume that there is a correlation between acceptable forms of language use and age.

The *linguistic* argument is that emojis offer a real affordance in language, and allow us to become better communicators, as written by the linguist Vyvyan Evans in his 2017 book *The Emoji Code*. He suggests that they can work as helpful non-verbal cues, allowing us to better express our emotions and attitudes in written language in more nuanced ways. These kinds of non-verbal cues – gesture, facial expressions, laughing, smiling, crying, and so on – are usually restricted to face-to-face, spoken channels of communication. Emojis therefore offer us a multi-modal system of communication, combining spoken and written forms of a language – or, as quoted above, to 'transcend linguistic borders'. Evans suggests that the use of emojis can help to avoid the 'angry jerk' phenomenon, which is when a person receives an email or other text-based form of digital communication, and it is misinterpreted with regards to the intended meaning. Emoji can add nuance to an expression, encoding non-verbal cues that would otherwise be missing.

A useful source of information where you can find more on emojis, technology and change is the *English and Media Centre*'s blog: www.cambridge.org/links/esccha6006, which also features an argument for teaching emojis in schools.

> **KEY TERM**
>
> **Multi-modal communication:** a way of communicating that uses multiple channels (e.g. speech and body language)

4 Language change

PRACTICE QUESTION

Attitudes to language change

Evaluate the following statement:

> Large numbers of intelligent people condemn and resent language change, regarding alterations as due to unnecessary sloppiness, laziness or ignorance (Aitchison 2012: 4)

In your answer, you could discuss:

- some of the different attitudes to language change
- the reasons why different attitudes exist
- particular examples or case studies of language change.

RESEARCH QUESTION
Evaluating articles about language

There are hundreds of opinion articles about language available online. Find around 20 articles, and for each one:

- Read it through and place it along a continuum, with 'prescriptivism' at one extreme and 'descriptivism' at the other. Briefly justify why you have placed it there.
- Consider the context of the article. What are the intended readership and the political stance of the publication? Is there a correlation here between these contextual factors and the position on the prescriptivist–descriptivist continuum?
- What are some of the more obvious metaphors for language used? For example, do they talk about language as if it were AN OBJECT TO BE DEFENDED, or as if it were A RESOURCE?

Although you shouldn't struggle to find articles, the following sources might be a good starting point:

- *The Telegraph*, April 2017: *The new £5 note has a major grammar blunder... But have you spotted it?*
- Oxford Dictionaries, November 2015: *Beyond words: how language-like is emoji?*
- *The Guardian*, May 2015: *ICYMI, English language is changing faster than ever, says expert.*

Wider reading

You can find out more about the topics in this chapter by reading the following:

Ideology, politics and language

Cameron, D. (1995). *Verbal Hygiene*. London: Routledge.

Milroy, J & Milroy, L. (2012). *Authority in Language*. London: Routledge.

Wardhaugh, R. (1999). *Proper English: Myths and Misunderstandings about Language*. Malden, MA: Wiley-Blackwell.

Attitudes to usage, variation and change

Curzan, A. (2016). *Fixing English: Prescriptivism and Language History*. Cambridge: Cambridge University Press.

Hitchings, H. (2011). *The Language Wars: A History of Proper English*. London: John Murray.

Kamm, O. (2015). *Accidence Will Happen: The Non-Pedantic Guide to English*. London: Weidenfeld & Nicolson.

Chapter 5
World Englishes

In this chapter, you will:

- Explore how and why English has become a global language
- Explore some varieties of World Englishes, and ways of classifying these
- Examine how different varieties of World Englishes come about
- Consider some of the issues related to language endangerment and death

World Englishes

So far this book has looked at change within the English language itself; this chapter now turns to large-scale changes in how and why English has spread around the world. It will consider the current conditions and varieties of World Englishes, some of the different attitudes towards these varieties, and what the consequences of this spread are for other languages. As you read through this chapter, it might be worth thinking back to Activity 2.4 in Chapter 2, where you explored different metaphors for English, such as ENGLISH IS A FOREST FIRE and ENGLISH IS A SPIDER WEB. This way of thinking and talking about World Englishes offers an interesting perspective on the way that English has 'moved' across the globe.

5.1 Defining World Englishes

English can truly be thought of as a global language – it is spoken by millions of people across hundreds of different countries, and is a language of international science, business and education. It is heard on television all over the world, and can be seen in signs, advertisements and menus in most of the places we travel to. In this section we will consider *why* this is the case. What is meant by a global language, and why do they exist? Do we talk about Englishes in the plural form? What does the presence of global languages mean for other languages? Why English? Will it always be a global language, or might this change in the future?

The terms *Global English*, *Globish*, *International English* and *World Englishes* have all been used to try and capture the enormity and complexity of English's global status. In this chapter, the term *World Englishes* will be adopted, because this recognises the existence of multiple varieties of English, rather than it just being one language that is used in uniform ways.

A language achieves global status when it develops a 'special role' that is widely recognised in a high number of countries around the world. This special role might exist due to the sheer number of native speakers – for English, this means in Britain, Ireland, the USA, Canada, Australia, New Zealand, South Africa, parts of the Caribbean and a number of other territories. Native speakers are those who are born and brought up speaking the language, in what is known as someone's L1 or 'first language'. Rough estimates, such as those by the *Ethnologue: Languages of the World* website (Simons and Fennig, 2017), place the number of native English speakers at around 372 million. But numbers of native speakers alone won't guarantee global status: other countries must take up the language and give it a special place, even though there may be few or no native speakers. This happens when a language is made an official language of a country, meaning that it is the medium of communication used by the government, the legal courts, the media and education. So, countries such as Jamaica, Singapore, Ghana and South Africa have multiple official languages, with English being one of them (see Figure 5.1).

Of course, native speakers are not the only people to use English. François Grosjean (2012) estimates that around half of the world's population is bilingual, meaning that

Language change

they don't just have an L1, but an L2 as well. For many people around the world, this L2 is English. It can also happen when a country decides to teach the language in schools, known as EFL (English as a Foreign Language). With a global language such as English, the picture is often complicated: it may exist alongside other official languages, and is very likely to be used as part of a speaker's multilingual inventory. Because of this complexity, numbers and statistics are difficult to acquire, but David Crystal (2003) estimates that nearly a quarter of the world's population are fluent or competent in English: a staggering 1.5 billion people.

> ### KEY TERMS
>
> **Global language:** a language that holds a 'special role' that is widely recognised in a high number of countries around the world
>
> **L1:** a speaker's first language
>
> **L2:** a speaker's second language
>
> **Official language:** a language used by a country in settings such as government, the legal courts, the media and education. Some countries recognise multiple official languages
>
> **EFL:** English as a Foreign Language, where English is taught as an L2 in schools

Figure 5.1: Countries (shown in green) where English is an official language

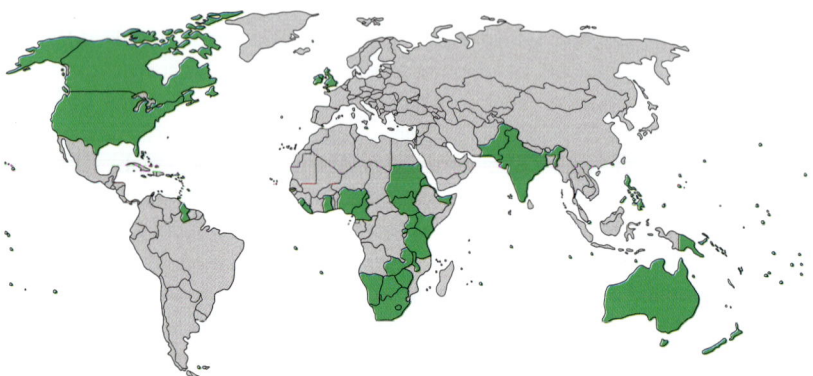

5.1.1 Why English?

A language becomes global not because of its linguistic properties or the number of speakers, but because of who those speakers are. Latin became a global language because of the rise and power of the Roman Empire. English became a global language because of British colonial expansion and Britain's industrial and trade power in the early nineteenth century. By the year 1900 the population of the USA was larger than any country in Western Europe, and its economy was the fastest growing in the world, catapulting English further around the world. These factors propelled English into the spotlight, increasing its number of speakers, yes, but more importantly – increasing its status. English was seen as highly desirable on the global business, education and media stage, and as international networks grew, so too did the need for a *lingua franca* (see Section 5.3.1). There is also the notion of prestige. Throughout history, Britain has held high political and economic influence, and is the language of the Western world. To be a fluent speaker of English is often seen as a passport to wealth, education, jobs and prosperity, but it also gives people access to Western culture, seen as desirable by many people all over the world. Note here the metaphor of LANGUAGE IS A KEY. Do you think this is an accurate way of thinking about language?

KEY TERM

Lingua franca: a language used as a contact language between speakers of different first languages

5.1.2 Language journeys

You have seen throughout this book that language and language change is often discussed through the use of metaphors, such as LANGUAGE IS A TRAVELLER, LANGUAGE IS A PHYSICAL OBJECT and LANGUAGE IS A PLANT. Focusing on one part of the world will help to demonstrate what is meant here. Take a look at the status of English in South Asia, the region which probably has the largest number of English speakers in the world (Crystal, 2003: 46). South Asian English has its roots in Britain, with the formation of the East India Company in 1600 – a group of English merchants who pursued trade links across South Asia. Its financial and political power grew across the region, especially during the British colonisation and control of India between 1765 and 1947. During this time, the English language also rose to prominence, becoming the language of government, administration, education and the social elite. When India gained independence in 1947, there were bitter and violent disputes about which language(s) should be used as the official – a difficult and politically charged task, given India's 900 million population and over 1000 languages. Hindi was chosen as the official language, with English as an 'associate language', and eighteen 'national languages' such as Urdu, Malayalam and Marathi. English remains a desirable and widely used language in South Asia, a lasting echo of the British colonisation of India and its influence throughout the region. Figures 5.2 and 5.3 are just two examples of the multilingual status of South Asia.

5 Language change

Figure 5.2: Shop sign in Mumbai, India – in English, Hindi and Gujarati

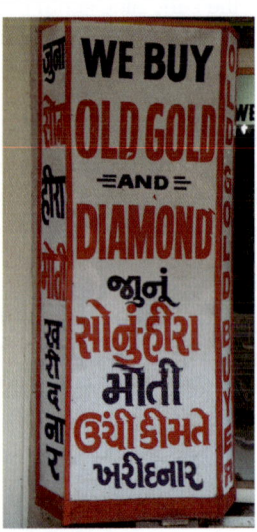

Figure 5.3: Sign in Jaffna, Sri Lanka – in Sinhala, Tamil and English

5.2 English around the world

Figure 5.4 is a map first published by Peter Strevens in 1980, which was one of the earliest attempts to show the global distribution of English. It shows the distribution of English from the two main branches, American English and British English.

Figure 5.4: English around the world

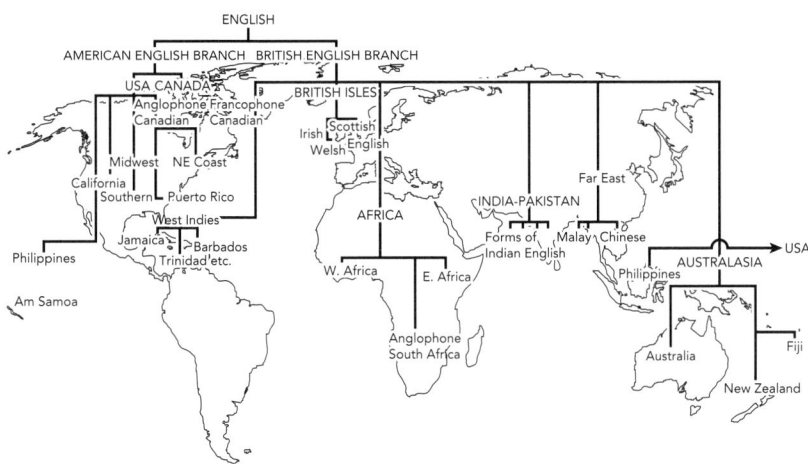

This map shows just how far English has reached around the world, but is fairly limited and one dimensional – it only shows us some of the places *where* English is used, not *how* it is used. Furthermore, the map only shows us a limited number of places where English is used as an L1 and L2. There are enormous parts of the world (e.g. South America) where, according to Strevens' map, English is not spoken at all – but this is obviously not the case. There are a number of other 'models' or ways of looking at World Englishes, some of which are explored in the following sections. You will see that modelling any global language is a difficult process, and there remains no satisfactory and complete way of doing so. Any model of a global language needs to take into account the political, social and linguistic complexities surrounding it. But, despite their limitations, models are a useful tool for exploring the different ways that English is used around the world. Before reading on, complete Activity 5.1.

ACTIVITY 5.1
Modelling World Englishes

Draw up a list of things you think it is important to know about World Englishes, and design a model to capture this information. You might want to think about the following:

- In your model, which variety is the reference point or 'standard' with which other varieties are compared? Why?

- What linguistic aspects would you be interested in capturing and including in your model?

5 Language change

- How will you ensure that your model does not suggest a hierarchy of varieties with 'better' and 'worse' varieties of World Englishes?
- Can you represent your model visually, using diagrams or maps?

5.2.1 The three circles model

A model of World Englishes was proposed by Braj Kachru in the 1980s and onwards, in what is known as the 'three circles model', reproduced in Figure 5.5.

Figure 5.5: Kachru's three circles model

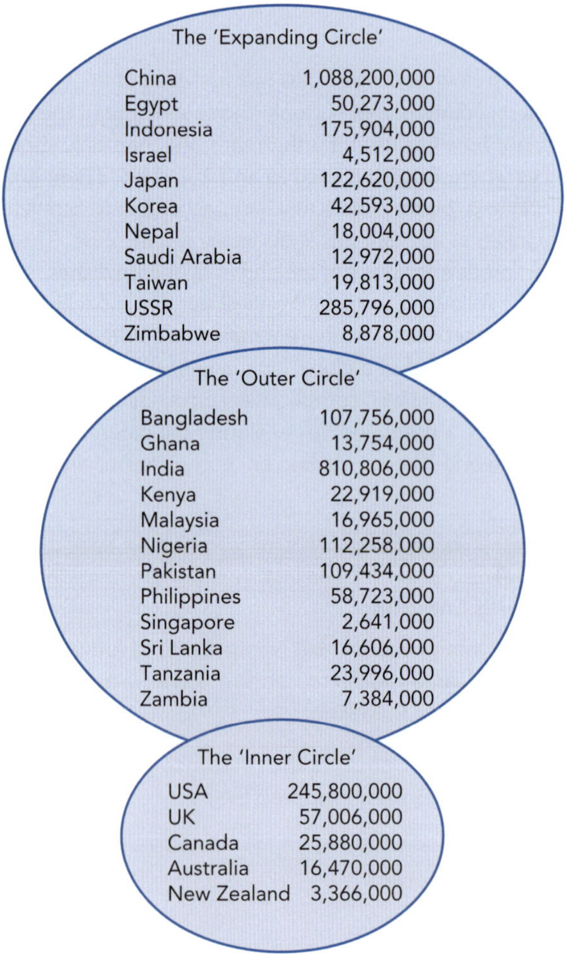

The 'Expanding Circle'

China	1,088,200,000
Egypt	50,273,000
Indonesia	175,904,000
Israel	4,512,000
Japan	122,620,000
Korea	42,593,000
Nepal	18,004,000
Saudi Arabia	12,972,000
Taiwan	19,813,000
USSR	285,796,000
Zimbabwe	8,878,000

The 'Outer Circle'

Bangladesh	107,756,000
Ghana	13,754,000
India	810,806,000
Kenya	22,919,000
Malaysia	16,965,000
Nigeria	112,258,000
Pakistan	109,434,000
Philippines	58,723,000
Singapore	2,641,000
Sri Lanka	16,606,000
Tanzania	23,996,000
Zambia	7,384,000

The 'Inner Circle'

USA	245,800,000
UK	57,006,000
Canada	25,880,000
Australia	16,470,000
New Zealand	3,366,000

Figure 5.5 gives numbers for whole populations rather than number of English speakers, which are now out of date. The three circles are:

- Expanding circle: parts of the world where English is recognised and used as an international language but does not have a colonial history. It is used for practical rather than cultural purposes, and often taught as an L2 (or L3 or L4).

- Outer circle: the earlier phases of the spread of English in non-native settings, where English is used as an L2. In these parts of the world, English is firmly established as an everyday language, is part of a country's political profile and an important second language.

- Inner circle: the traditional bases of English, where it is used as an L1.

Kachru's model is useful in some senses: it shows that English is used for different purposes around the world and gives us an idea of how it operates within multilingual contexts. But the model was devised in the 1980s, and despite its popularity it is perhaps not an accurate representation of what present-day World English looks like. Indeed, David Crystal (2003: 60) suggests that a more appropriate term for 'expanding circle' would be 'expanded circle', to reflect the fact that English is recognised and used virtually everywhere. Furthermore, not all varieties of English will fit neatly into one of the three circles, and the model is limited in that it doesn't show the diversity *within* each circle, or the boundaries between circles. Because the model is based on geography rather than the way speakers use and identify with English, information about multilingualism is missing: many English speakers grow up speaking more than one language, using different languages to fulfil different social functions. The model has also been criticised for its rather prescriptivist labels, as 'outer' and 'inner' seem to suggest 'better' and 'worse' varieties.

5.2.2 McArthur's circle of World Englishes

Tom McArthur's 1987 circular model (seen in Figure 5.6) places 'World Standard English' at its centre, from which all other varieties are derived. The next layer shows regional varieties, which includes standard and standardizing forms (where 'standardizing' means undergoing a process of standardization). The outer layer divides the world into eight regions, described by McArthur as a 'crowded (even riotous) fringe of sub-varieties such as Aboriginal English, Black English *Vernacular, Gullah*, Jamaican Nation Language, Singapore English and Ulster Scots'.

5 Language change

Figure 5.6: McArthur's circle of World Englishes

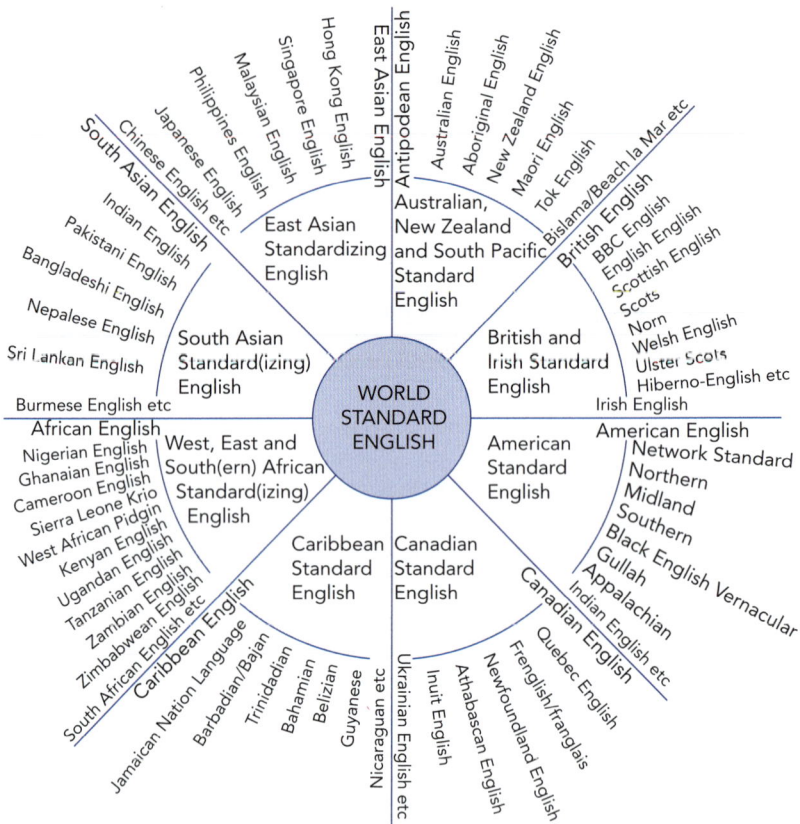

Although McArthur's model is more detailed than Strevens' map or Kachru's circles, it is still limited and doesn't recognise the complexities of multilingualism. And it shares the same problem with data of this sort in that it becomes quickly outdated, especially when dealing with a concept that changes rapidly.

5.2.3 Schneider's dynamic model

A more recent attempt to capture the complexities of World Englishes was proposed by Edgar Schneider in 2007. His *dynamic model* accounts for the nature of language contact, which you will explore further in Section 5.3. This is a particularly useful way of looking at global change because it shows how languages co-exist with one another (either at peace or in conflict), rather than simply existing as varieties by themselves that bear no relation to each other. The model is detailed and tracks changes in language and society over a number of years, beginning with the process of colonisation. Underlying the theory is an evolutionary metaphor to explain language change, suggesting that language evolves as a process of 'competition and selection'. The case of English

World Englishes

in India, as discussed earlier, is a particularly good example of the model in action. Schneider proposes 5 'phases' of global change, attempting to describe sociolinguistic conditions and how languages are affected structurally within each of these. They can be summarised as follows:

- **Phase 1, *Foundation*.** This phase is when English is brought in to a country where it was not previously used, normally by English speaking settlers. Here there is likely to be tension between settlers and indigenous groups, as they see themselves distinct from one another and tend to communicate within their own confines. A bilingual community emerges.

- **Phase 2, *Exonormative stabilisation*.** As English begins to have more influence, two varieties co-exist: the settler strand and the indigenous group strand. This phase sees the gradual movement of the settler variety towards the indigenous variety, as local vocabulary is incorporated, code-switching occurs and English starts to be seen as an asset.

- **Phase 3, *Nativisation*.** The most important and dynamic phase, which sees the establishment of a new identity as the gap between settler and indigenous varieties is reduced. There is increasing pressure on indigenous speakers to acquire English. At a linguistic level, there are significant changes in the phonology, lexis and grammar of English.

- **Phase 4, *Endonormative stabilisation*.** This is when the new variety becomes gradually accepted as the local norm, moving towards a linguistic homogeneity. Members of the settler groups start to see themselves as part of the 'new nation', and ethnic boundaries are redefined for indigenous groups.

- **Phase 5, *Differentiation*.** The new variety reflects local culture and identity. More local varieties of English develop, perhaps as settler and indigenous groups seek to re-establish their ethnic heritage.

5.2.4 Classifying varieties by prestige

One further way of classifying language varieties is to use a sociolinguistic criterion, based on the kind of attitudes and types of prestige that speakers hold towards a particular variety. To understand this, it is useful to consider the difference between William Labov's 1972 terms covert and overt prestige.

> **KEY TERMS**
>
> **Covert prestige:** where local, vernacular varieties are positively valued in subversive and subconscious ways
>
> **Overt prestige:** where varieties to be valued are publicly and explicitly recommended by powerful institutions and social groups, and are seen as socially desirable

5 Language change

- In covert prestige, local, vernacular varieties are positively valued, emphasising community 'togetherness' and local identity. The word *covert* is used because prestige is usually demonstrated subconsciously between members of a group.

- In overt prestige, varieties to be valued are publicly and explicitly recommended by powerful institutions and social groups, and are seen as socially desirable.

So, different varieties can have different levels of prestige, depending on their status within a local and global speech community. For example, a dying language that is rapidly losing speakers may be held in low prestige by speakers who have abandoned the language in favour of another, higher prestige variety. Of course, the speakers who still use the dying language may feel exactly the same way about the bigger language, and view the dying language as the more prestigious form. Varieties may also be stigmatised by outsiders and given labels such as 'crude' and 'ugly', but actually have covert prestige status, where speakers are seen to be warm, tough, fashionable or humorous. For example, Jamaican Creole and American Vernacular English are often seen as inferior and not 'proper' forms of a language. Then there are standard or near-standard varieties of World Englishes (such as Standard Singaporean English and Nigerian Standard English) that carry overt prestige labels, with speakers being seen as powerful, cultured and polite and educated. Finally, there are varieties that carry global overt prestige – typically British Standard English spoken with a Received Pronunciation accent and US Standard English spoken with a General American accent. Such attitudes are pervasive throughout the world, both in countries where English is and isn't an official language. For example, consider the message in Figure 5.7, a poster produced in September 2017 by the Američki Institut, a centre for the promotion of American culture based in the Croatian capital of Zagreb. Melania Trump, who is shown on the poster, was born in the region. What does it reveal about attitudes to language and what they mean?

Figure 5.7: English language school advert

ACTIVITY 5.2
Evaluating the models

Critically evaluate the different models of World Englishes. What are the advantages/disadvantages of each? How do they compare with one another? Which one, in your opinion, offers the most ideal model? Do you have any suggestions for how the models might be improved so that they are more relevant for today's world?

5.2.5 A continuum of speech forms

In many societies, there is a continuum of speech forms – from a standard variety typically used in formal contexts through to a non-standard variety typically used in informal contexts. The labels acrolect, mesolect and basilect can be used for the 'high', 'middle' and 'low' points of the continuum, as shown on Figure 5.8.

Figure 5.8: Speech forms

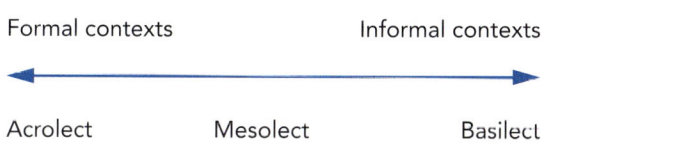

These labels are generally used when describing pidgin and creole forms. What is useful about these labels is that they recognise the fact that context affects how people use language. So, the same person may use the acrolect form at work but switch to the mesolect or basilect form when at home or with friends. In terms of their linguistic properties, extreme ends of the continuum are the most different from one other, so an acrolect and a basilect are the most linguistically remote from each other.

KEY TERMS

Acrolect: a prestigious or standard variety of a language

Mesolect: an intermediate prestigious variety of a language

Basilect: a low prestigious variety of a language

5 Language change

5.3 Language contact

You have seen how and why English has spread far and wide around the world, and you will look at what happens when English 'bumps into' other languages, in a process known as language contact. Mixed varieties involving English are often given nicknames to reflect their intermingled nature – Chinglish, Spanglish, Singlish, Franglais, Tex-Mex, and many more. Indeed, it may be more useful to think of languages 'meshing' together rather than just coming into 'contact'. Contact has substantial consequences for the historical development of the languages involved: borrowing words from other languages, changes in phonology and grammar, a general increase in bilingualism and the creation of pidgins and creoles. Most languages around the world have some form of contact with one another – it is very rare that a group of speakers exist in a completely isolated environment with no contact with other linguistic communities.

English is often described as a *scavenger language*, taking words from other languages that it comes into contact with. It has also lost words, such as the ones it has given up from Old English in favour of words from French, Latin, Greek, Turkish, Hindi – the list goes on and on. After British colonisers originally exported the language around the world, migration has brought English 'back' to Britain in a variety of altered forms. In these linguistic cocktails, used predominantly in large cities, speakers of non-British heritages have blended their L1 speech patterns with existing local dialects. The result is a vast array of fabulous new varieties of English, such as London Jamaican English and Bradford Asian English. British English itself has also been developed and enriched by an explosion of new terms, such as *balti* (a type of curry invented in Birmingham, which would translate as 'bucket' in Urdu, Hindi and Bengali) and *bhangra* (traditional Punjabi music mixed with reggae and hip-hop).

KEY TERM

Language contact: a process of language change whereby multiple languages come into social contact and have linguistic influence on each other, in the form of borrowings, grammatical and phonological change, formation of pidgins and creoles, and higher rates of bilingualism

5.3.1 English as a *lingua franca*

A *lingua franca* is a language used between speakers who have no common language between them, to enable communication for purposes such as trade. *Lingua francas* are built on a base language, which tends to be a global language such as English, for obvious reasons. Thus, English is the world's most common *lingua franca*, and Arabic, French, Hindi, Portuguese, Spanish, Swahili and several others are also used in this way. A *lingua franca* is often described as an 'auxiliary' language, used for functional rather than social purposes, and speakers are just as likely to be native users as they are non-native. It is a convenient method of communication to serve global human relations, and is appreciated by millions worldwide. Jennifer Jenkins (2006) lists five common characteristics of English as a lingua franca:

1. It provides a mutually intelligible language, used by speakers of different languages allowing them to communicate with one another.
2. It is an alternative to English as a Foreign Language, rather than a replacement – it serves a functional communicative purpose rather than being associated with education.
3. It is just as likely to include elements of Standard English as well as linguistic features reflective of more local forms.
4. Accommodation and code switching are common practice during *lingua franca* communication.
5. Language proficiency in speakers may be low or high.

In terms of the linguistic structure of English as a *lingua franca*, Barbara Seidlhofer (2011) identifies the following typical characteristics:

- non-use of the third-person present tense –s (e.g. *she look very sad*)

- interchangeable use of the relative pronouns *who* and *which* (e.g. *a book who*; *a person which*)

- omission of the definite (*the*) and indefinite articles (*a/an*) where they are obligatory in native speaker English and insertion where they do not occur in native speaker English

- use of an all-purpose question tag such as *isn't it?* or *no?* instead of *shouldn't they?* (e.g. *they should arrive soon, isn't it?*)

- increasing of redundancy by adding prepositions (e.g. *we have to study about*) or by increasing explicitness (*blue colour* vs. *blue* and *how long time?* vs. *how long?*)

Language change

- heavy reliance on certain verbs of high semantic generality, such as *do*, *have*, *make*, *put* and *take*

- pluralisation of nouns which are considered uncountable in native speaker English (e.g. *informations*, *staffs*, *advices*)

- use of *that*-clauses instead of infinitive constructions (e.g. *I want that we discuss about my essay*).

These characteristics demonstrate that English is shaped as much by its non-native speakers as by its native speakers. However, many people adopt the rather prescriptive view that *lingua francas* are somehow inferior or deficient forms of a language, with crude and basic grammatical and phonological systems. Jenkins (2007) discusses the implications of this – that there can be a bias against non-native forms such as *lingua francas*, because of a preference for the 'correct' native forms of English. She argues that speakers should have a choice about the forms they use, and that the use of standard, native forms is unnecessary for most of the world's English speakers.

5.3.2 Types of contact

Language contact is common and one of the main reasons for language change. For example, English has borrowed extensively from French, Greek and other languages throughout the course of history. Indigenous languages in Papua New Guinea, the Amazon and Australia have changed as a result of contact with other, non-native forms. In the Balkans, different languages such as Albanian, Bulgarian and Greek all share certain features of lexis, grammar and phonology due to sustained contact and convergence.

Linguists differentiate between superstratum, substratum and adstratum contact situations. In superstratal contact, the language of a socially powerful group influences the language of the less powerful. This type of contact is common in post-colonial contexts, with words from the colonisers' language finding their way into the language of the colonised, or replacing the indigenous language completely. Substratal contact is the reverse: when a dominant language is influenced by a less dominant one. This often happens when the less dominant language is losing speakers, such as the influence of Irish upon the English spoken in Ireland. Adstratal contact is where two (or more) languages come into contact, but there is no dominant community. This often happens with neighbouring languages.

World Englishes

> **KEY TERMS**
>
> **Superstratum:** a type of language contact where the language of a more powerful group influences the language of a less powerful group
>
> **Substratum:** a type of language contact where the language of a less powerful group influences the language of a more powerful group
>
> **Adstratum:** a type of language contact where there is no dominant language

5.4 Language birth: pidgins and creoles

Whereas a *lingua franca* is typically a language with a broad base of native speakers that share the same language family, when people from different parts of the world meet they do not often have such a language in common. Instead, the two (or more) groups use their native languages as a basis for a new, rudimentary language of reduced vocabulary and grammatical rules, in what is called a pidgin. When a pidgin becomes so well established that it becomes the mother-tongue of a speech community (when children are brought up speaking it), it becomes a creole.

5.4.1 Case study: Nigerian Pidgin English

Nigerian Pidgin English has its origins in trade contact between the British and locals in the 1800s, and is spoken widely in large cities and ports in south Nigeria. Throughout history Nigerian Pidgin English was associated with non-educated people and perceived negatively by the educated, however in recent years there has been a shift in its status: it is now widespread among the educated, used by young people, musicians and writers, and perceived by many as 'more Nigerian' than English. It also serves as a social identity, when speakers want to emphasise their *Nigerian* identity as opposed to their ethnic group identity. So, Nigerian Pidgin English is advantageous in that it can express a sense of belonging to Nigeria, which English, the language of the ex-colonial power, cannot.

Although no official status has been granted to Nigerian Pidgin English in Nigeria, many people have suggested it would be a good candidate for a national language largely due to its identity marking function. However, the language is not yet developed enough to satisfy all the duties of a national language: there is no standard spelling system due to its little use as a written form, and for many people it still carries negative connotations of being uneducated. Text 5A is an example of what Nigerian Pidgin English looks like, along with its English transcription.

5 Language change

Text 5A

How bodi? / How you dey?	How are you doing today?
Wetin dey happen?	What's going on?
Comot for road	Make way/get out of my way
I wan chop	I want to eat
Dem send you?	Did they send you?

5.4.2 Case study: Tok Pisin

Tok Pisin is an English-based creole widely used in Papua New Guinea, where it is classified as an official language (along with English). It has around 4 million speakers (combining L1 and L2 speakers), making it the most widely used of the 750 or so languages used in the country, including English. It is widely regarded as the most developed pidgin-creole in the world, with a standardised grammar and spelling system. English is the superstratal language, but Tok Pisin is also influenced by Tolai (an indigenous language of Papua New Guinea), German, Samoan and various other local languages. Christian missionaries first brought English to the island in the 1600s in an attempt to convert the local population, and the whaling trade in the 1700s introduced even more contact. Despite the fact that it is historically based on English, over time Tok Pisin has transformed into a language in its own right. Text 5B is an example of what it looks like, and its English translation.

Text 5B

Wanpela taim rokrok i bin save stap klostu long wara. Em i bin naispela na em i save wok hat. Rokrok i bin save stap em wanpela tasol. Na em i bin tingting long painim wanpela man bilong en. Long maunten klostu long wara wanpela snek i save stap. Em i naispela snek. Long dispela taim snek i gat lek olsem ol narapela animal.

Once upon a time a frog used to live near a river/water. She was beautiful and she was in the habit of working hard. Frog was living alone. And she decided to look for a husband. On a hill near the lake lived a snake. He was a handsome snake. At that time snakes had legs like other animals.

World Englishes

ACTIVITY 5.3
Linguistic properties of pidgins and creoles

Examine the examples of pidgin and creole in Texts 5A and 5B and analyse the lexical, grammatical and phonological properties of each one. You might want to think about:

- Grammar: Are there any grammatical words that are missing or added? If so, what kinds of words are these? What grammatical rules have been retained/adapted from English?

- Semantics: Have any words changed/adapted their meaning? How?

- Phonology: How have speech sounds been affected? Can you find any significant patterns of sound change?

5.5 Language endangerment and death

English is just one of the many thousands of languages in the world, and recent estimates by *Ethnologue*, the largest present-day survey of world languages, put the total number at somewhere between 5,000 and 6,000. But whatever the true number may be, it is a number that is decreasing rapidly. The rise of a global language may bring benefits, but it also brings dangers, and linguists studying endangered languages (e.g. Nettle and Romaine, 2000) suggest that 90 per cent of the world's languages are expected to disappear by 2100. The most looming threat to such endangered languages is the rise of global languages. A very small number of languages account for a vast proportion of the world's population (over 7.3 billion people), and the 8 languages with over 100 million speakers (Mandarin, Spanish, English, Bengali, Hindi, Portuguese, Russian, Japanese) have around 2.5 billion speakers between them. Looking at all the world's languages, 96 per cent of them are spoken by just 4 per cent of the world's population.

5.5.1 How and why do languages die?

What is language death, and what are the reasons that a language would die? Larry Trask (1994: 69) defines language death as where 'people abandon their language in favour of some other language seen as more prestigious or useful'. In short then, a language dies when nobody speaks it any more. One possibility is that all its speakers might die – through natural causes, or, more likely, killed by more powerful neighbours. For example, when the British arrived

5 Language change

in Tasmania in 1803 they found that the native people rather got in the way of their plans for settlement, and so ordered them out of their own territory and killed anybody who tried to resist. It is reported that the last living native, a 64-year-old woman called Truganini who died in 1876, spoke not a single word of English.

Language death doesn't have to involve such violent means, but read any book about language endangerment and you will find plenty of violent metaphors: some people talk of 'language murder' and 'language suicide', suggesting that languages do not die natural deaths, but are rather killed by other languages, drawing on the metaphor of A LANGUAGE IS A PERSON. English has been described as one of these 'language killers', as seems to be the case in the Tasmanian example just cited. But of course a language itself can't be a killer, so are such emotive and loaded terms really that useful, or are they harmful and potentially dangerous? To understand language death, it is important to consider local and global contexts, and examine the types of human behaviour that lead to it.

Speakers of a language often abandon their native tongue in favour of another, that is seen as more prestigious or powerful, in a process called language shift. Many people see English as one of these more prestigious and powerful languages, and there are many examples of speakers abandoning their own language in favour of it. But why does English hold such prestige? It certainly isn't anything to do with the language itself, and there's no reason that the vocabulary, grammar and phonology of English contributes to its prestige. No language is inherently superior to another, rather it is the associations of the language that make it so popular: English is the most widely used language of the internet, the language of much international trade, the language of international culture (such as the Hollywood film industry), and much, much more. In short, it is not languages themselves that 'kill' other languages: it is when a politically, economically and culturally powerful society imposes itself on a less powerful one.

Hans-Jürgen Sasse (1992) proposed a model of 'language shift' to demonstrate what processes are at work when languages are endangered. It is simplified here in Figure 5.9.

> **KEY TERM**
>
> **Language shift:** a term used to describe a speaker's / speech community's sudden or gradual shift from the use of one language to another

World Englishes

Figure 5.9: Sasse's model of language shift (1992)

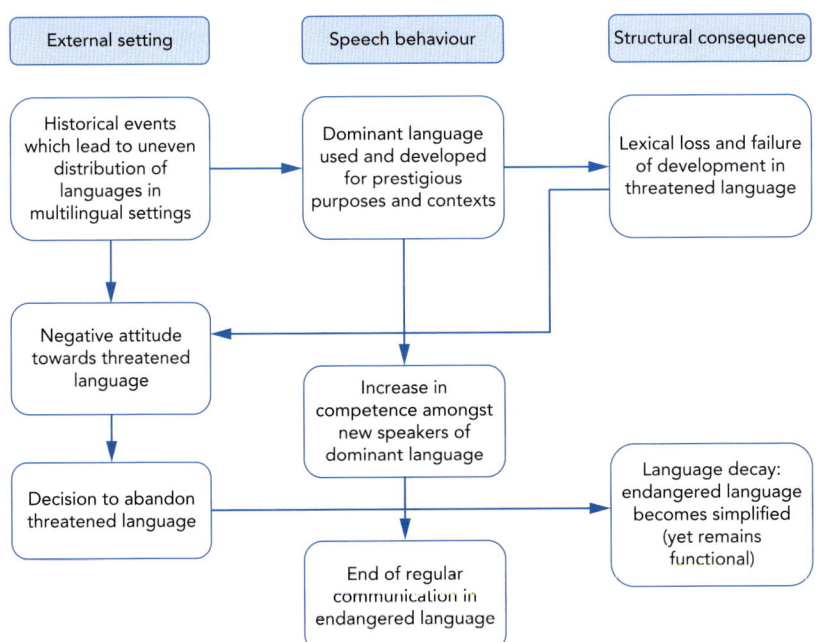

5.5.2 Should we care?

In short, yes. Languages carve the world up in very different ways, and languages offer a window into the human mind. Language reveals the many creative ways in which humans organise and categorise their experience. For linguists, the preservation of languages may seem to appear a little self-serving. Linguists need to study as many languages as possible to refine theories of language structure and to train future generations of linguists. There are new and exciting discoveries about languages still being made, and there is every reason to believe that what is now known about language is just the tip of the iceberg. Diversity is good for the human race – it allows us to express identity, community and celebrates difference. In linguistics, such celebration of diversity is known as peace linguistics, a movement that seeks to promote peace and human rights by emphasising the value of language diversity and multilingualism.

KEY TERM

Peace linguistics: an approach to linguistics that emphasises the value of language diversity and the need to respect the dignity of individual speakers and speech communities

5 Language change

The rise of global languages can be good in that it increases levels of communication and shared understanding around the world. A global language is an incredible world resource which opens up plentiful opportunities for multicultural communication, mutual understanding and shared co-operation. It can help to create advancements in science, education and politics, and can make exploring the world easier, in some senses. But the rise of a global language means that smaller languages suffer – and are threatened with extinction. A major reason that languages become endangered is because of the threat of global languages such as English.

> **PRACTICE QUESTION**
> Linguistic jingoism
> Text 5C is a screenshot of an online petition that surfaced in June 2016, shortly after Britain voted to leave the European Union. What kinds of attitudes towards language does this text show?

Text 5C

5.6 Do we need global languages?

It is often suggested that we need global languages to communicate in our modern 'global village', particularly for trade, education, politics and international travel. Large global bodies such as the United Nations, the World Bank and the World Health Organization depend on global languages for efficient and economic communication. Global languages are undeniably useful, and allow us to communicate with an increasing range of speakers from diverse backgrounds. Countries may well choose to adapt a global language for economic reasons and to be seen as more 'credible' by others.

But we have seen the dangers and impact a global language can have on other languages, as well as cultural identity. People have a natural desire to use their mother-tongue and to see it flourish, and do not react well when an alternative language is forced or imposed upon them. Many speakers may have no desire to be part of a 'global village'. But to reject a global language in favour of a local language is often seen as a risk – if a community chooses to use English, they have a greater chance of accessing global amenities; but this means sacrificing aspects of their cultural and linguistic identity. Language is political and global languages often have a rather unsavoury history, due to associations of colonial violence, pressure and oppression. Global language speakers have a responsibility to understand and celebrate the nature of linguistic diversity, to respect people's linguistic choices and to be aware of the power that speaking a global language has.

RESEARCH QUESTION
Investigating Englishes

This research task asks you to investigate a range of World Englishes. Prepare a report, presentation or case study about a particular global variety of English. If you are working in groups, then it might be useful to each take a variety from the 'outer', 'inner' and 'expanding' circles by Braj Kachru. You should include the following elements:

- How the particular variety came about – its roots and its history

- Number of L1/L2 speakers, where it is spoken, and its status as an official/unofficial language

- How it has been shaped by language contact

- What type of prestige (e.g. covert/overt) it carries across different local/global social groups, and why

- Some of its phonological and grammatical properties, and in what ways these are similar/different to British English.

5 Language change

Wider reading

Read more about World Englishes by exploring the following books:

Crystal, D. (2003). *English as a Global Language*. Cambridge: Cambridge University Press.

Saraceni, M. (2015). *World Englishes: A Critical Analysis*. London: Bloomsbury.

Schneider, E. (2011). *English Around the World: An Introduction*. Cambridge: Cambridge University Press.

Ideas and answers

Chapter 1

Activity 1.1
These statements are designed to be rather contentious and provoke debate. Of course, there is no one 'correct' answer but, as with all work with language, a descriptivist view should ultimately be agreed on. An important aspect to consider for all statements is context; for example, discussions around statement g. could come to the conclusion that a more accurate term for 'correct' language use should be 'appropriate' language use. You could also discuss how language use is tied up with wider ideological issues, as implied in h. and i.

Activity 1.2
After doing this activity, it should be clear that people belong to multiple speech communities that overlap with one another. Different speech communities draw on different linguistic repertoires, according to the context and situation of use.

Chapter 2

Activity 2.1
You could make use of an Old English dictionary to help with this activity. There are a number of these available online, such as: old-engli.sh/dictionary.php. The text is about God creating things in the universe: the sun (*sunne*), the moon (*mona*) and various animals such as whales (*hwalas*), fish (*fisccynn*) and serpents (*wyrmcynn*). The most obvious pattern is the 'on the [number] day' (*on ðam* [number] *dæe*).

Activity 2.2
a   The writer of the poem clearly feels strongly about the way that English and French are used. English is seen as the 'low status' variety, French as the 'high status' variety. This reflects some of the linguistic attitudes that were present during the ME period.

b   Both groups were probably fiercely proud of their language but recognised the fact that different languages held different levels of prestige. Many Norman invaders wished to impose their language onto native speakers, in an act of power that would force English speakers to 'conform'. Many native English speakers wished to resist this change, staying true to their English linguistic identity.

Language change

c   The ME period was a time of great social change and language contact, meaning people probably held fairly strong views about language. If a native English speaker adopted the Norman language, it may have been perceived as 'giving in' to the invaders and losing a sense of 'Englishness'.

d   Attitudes to language use, variation and change are *never* just about language. The language you choose to speak – or not speak – can reveal a lot about identity and nationhood. The pride that English and Norman societies had about their language is nothing strange, and the same kind of attitudes are of course in existence today.

Activity 2.3

Below is a 2009 translation of this passage by the poet Simon Armitage.

> In a strange region he scales steep slopes;
>
> far from his friends he cuts a lonely figure.
>
> Where he bridges a brook or wades through a waterway
>
> ill fortune brings him face to face with a foe
>
> so foul or fierce he is bound to use force.
>
> So momentous are his travels among the mountains
>
> to tell just a tenth would be a tall order.
>
> Here he scraps with serpents and snarling wolves,
>
> here he tangles with wodwos causing trouble in the crags,
>
> or with bulls and bears and the odd wild boar.
>
> Hard on his heels through the highlands come giants.
>
> Only diligence and faith in the face of death
>
> will keep him from becoming a corpse or carrion.

Some ideas might include:

- Adjective position: in the original, adjectives often appear before the noun: e.g. *contrayez straunge*. In the modern version, the reverse is true: e.g. *strange region*.

- Change in writing system: loss of the letters <ȝ> and <þ>.

- A more phonetically rendered spelling system: the /z/ at the end of *rydez*, *bullez* and *berez* reflects pronunciation more accurately than PDE *rides*, *bulls* and *bears*.

Ideas and answers

- Loss of *wars* as a verb: this appears as *werrez* in the original, but PDE usually uses words such as *fights* or *scraps* (as in the translation provided).

Activity 2.4

Some of the metaphors construe English as a physical object (e.g. ENGLISH IS A SPONGE, ENGLISH IS A WEAPON). Some construe a particular political agenda, such as in ENGLISH IS A WEAPON and ENGLISH IS A CURRENCY, where English is seen to be used as a tool for gaining political, social or financial advantage over others. Some metaphors reveal the way that English has 'spread' around the world, such as ENGLISH IS A FOREST FIRE and ENGLISH IS A SPIDER WEB. Of course, none of the metaphors are 'accurate', confirming the idea that it is incredibly difficult to talk about language *without* using metaphor.

This kind of activity could easily be turned into a larger-scale project, looking at different metaphors in real texts about the English language.

Chapter 3

Activity 3.1

The obvious thing to notice here is that language change is heavily affected by sociocultural changes and technological developments. For example, the result from the <analogue, digital> search reveals peaks and troughs of a word's usage over time. *Fax* is an interesting case, rising sharply in the 1980s but falling again in the mid-2000s as a result of new communication technologies such as email. Of course, *email* itself is a shortening from *electronic mail*. Students could try searching for these two terms, to see how their usage compares against each other.

Activity 3.2

Those that do not have access to the OED website could analyse the word formation of the following words, which were added to the dictionary in September 2017:

- augmentee
- cheeselog
- chronozone
- smartphone app
- online dater
- e-book reader
- funky-ass
- gosht

Activity 3.3

Recordings should be made in a quiet environment, free from background noise. Ideally, the speech samples should be taken from naturally occurring dialogue. Points (1) and (2) are focused on vowel sounds, and are likely to be affected by the regional origin of the speaker. Point (4) is a phonetic feature that is found throughout the UK.

Language change

Chapter 4

Activity 4.1

The third option in this activity is to practise what Rob Pope (1995) calls *textual intervention*, where an original text (the 'base' text) is reimagined as something different. The choices of new texts are endless, but should be critical of the prescriptive view of language that is evident in the base text. The commentary is designed to provide a space to reflect on language choices, explaining and justifying why certain choices were made.

Activity 4.2

Sadly, many of the views found online about uptalk are highly prescriptive, reflecting a deep misunderstanding of what language is. These prescriptive views also relate to a much wider philosophical problem: What gives people the idea that they have the right to criticise other people's language choices? Prescriptive values of language are deeply embedded in society, and are often not helped by the media. Even 'liberal' publications such as *The Guardian* are guilty of holding prescriptive views about language. The most 'extreme' prescriptive views, however, are likely to be found in conservative publications such as *The Daily Mail*.

Activity 4.3

Out of the 19 words, the words chosen as a result of technological change are: *podcast*; *carbon-neutral*; *carbon footprint*; *unfriend*; *GIF*; *selfie*; *vape* and 😂. This means that 42% of the OED words of the year were chosen because of technological changes. Many of them follow typical word-formation patterns: for example, *unfriend* is an example of affixation; *podcast* is an example of blending (*iPod* + *broadcast*).

Practice question

This statement, from Jean Aitchison, is designed to be used as a springboard for exploring a range of attitudes towards language change. Answers might include:

- The descriptive/prescriptive dichotomy

- Acknowledging the fact that language operates within sociocultural contexts, and that change is a product of this

- Metaphors of change, such as those proposed throughout the course of the book, and by Aitchison herself (see Section 4.3.1)

- Various myths about language change, such as the idea that change is due to 'laziness'

Ideas and answers

- Reasons for attitudes to change: how views about language are often tied up with wider sociocultural factors such as politics and education
- Arguments for the reconceptualisation of 'correct' language to notions of 'appropriateness' and 'register'.

Chapter 5

Activity 5.1

This is a challenging activity and you will need to think about the complexities and sensitivities of designing a model of a world language. You might need to make some controversial or unpopular decisions, such as having Standard English grammar and Received Pronunciation as the 'standard' or reference point to which all other varieties are compared. Any model of world language should undoubtedly include details about the lexicon, the grammatical and phonological structure, and the various global varieties – though it is, of course, difficult to design a system that can capture all of this. Number of speakers might also be an important piece of information to include. Remember not to think in terms of 'good' or 'bad' varieties, and that diagrams/maps can be a useful way of representing this.

Activity 5.2

None of the models discussed in this chapter is perfect. The following table presents some of the strengths and weaknesses of each.

	Strengths	Weaknesses
Kachru	This was the first model of World Englishes and it triggered a surge of research interest in this area.	It is a hierarchical model, where the outer and expanding circles seem to be 'less-good' varieties of English. It suggests a simplified version of how English exists alongside other languages.
McArthur	It does not present a 'core' regional variety of English at its centre, meaning that there is no suggestion of one variety being 'better' than another.	It is unclear in what it means by 'World Standard English'. It does not account for areas where English is used as a *lingua franca*.

Language change

	Strengths	Weaknesses
Schneider	It accounts for the dynamic, diachronic nature of language contact and change. It is a sociocultural model of World Englishes, accounting for multilingual contexts.	It is an oversimplification of what constitutes linguistic identity. It appears to suggest that it is synonymous with national identity, which is often not the case. See Mesthrie and Bhatt (2008: 35–6) for a detailed criticism.

Activity 5.3
Text 5A
Grammar

- Omission of auxiliary verb *be* in constructions such as *how you dey, wetin dey happen* and *dem send you*

- Omission of preposition *to* in *I wan chop*

- No progressive aspect marking on *happen*

- Retention of Subject-Verb-Object word order

Semantics

- *Chop* stands in for *eat*, which has obvious semantic associations

Phonology

- Clipping of word-initial sounds such as *everybody* → *bodi* and *today* → *dey*

- *Comot* is a variation of *come out*, where the original diphthong /au/ is changed to a short vowel /o/

- th-stopping: where the dental fricative /ð/ changes to an alveolar stop such as /d/, as in *them* → *dey/them*

Text 5B
Grammar

- The word order is roughly the same as English (Subject-Verb-Object). If determiners are present, then they appear before nouns (e.g. *other animal* → *narapela animal*), but are often omitted completely

- Adjectives can be attributive (*naispela snek*) or predicative (*em i bin naispela*)

Ideas and answers

Semantics

- Some words are markedly different from their English counterparts (e.g. *naispela* means handsome; *stap* means *live*)

- *rokrok* means *frog* and has an onomatopoeic root

- *wara* refers to a body of water: e.g. *lake*, *river*

Phonology

- Diphthongs are often changed to short vowels (e.g. /ei/ → /e/ in *snake* → *snek*)

- Assimilation processes have formed separate words in Tok Pisin, where in English there would be two, e.g. *close to* → *klostu*

- *Tingting* derives from English *thinking*, with an example of th-stopping (the dental fricative /θ/ changes to the alveolar stop /t/), which is also used to mean *decide, thoughts, forget* or other general verbs of cognition

For a useful Tok Pisin–English dictionary, see www.tok-pisin.com/sort-tokpisin.php

Practice question

You might include some of the following ideas in your answer:

- The deep irony of the statement, given that English has borrowed extensively from French over the course of history.

- The view and attitude towards language projected in this text. Is it prescriptive or descriptive?

- The views that the text projects about the 'ownership' of language. How could you explore the metaphor of LANGUAGE IS A PHYSICAL OBJECT to discuss the way that people talk about 'owning', 'stealing' and 'borrowing' language?

- The fact that language change is inevitable, and proposed 'interventions' such as this are flawed from the outset.

- Wider implications about linguistic identity, nationalism and racism.

International Phonetic Alphabet (IPA) chart

Consonants				Vowels	
				Short vowels	
p	pip	ŋ	sing	ɪ	pit
b	bib	l	let	e	pet
t	ten	r	ride	æ	pat
d	den	w	wet	ɒ	pot
k	cat	j	yet	ʌ	but
g	get			ʊ	book
f	fish			ə	mother
v	voice			Long vowels	
θ	thigh			iː	bean
ð	this			ɜː	burn
s	set			ɑː	barn
z	zoo			ɔː	born
ʃ	ship			uː	boon
ʒ	measure			Diphthongs	
h	hen			aɪ	bite	eɪ	bait
tʃ	church			ɔɪ	boy	əʊ	toe
dʒ	judge			aʊ	house	ʊə	cure
m	man			ɪə	ear	eə	air
n	now				

References

Aitchison, J. (1996). 'A web of worries'. *The Reith Lectures*. BBC. Available at: www.bbc.co.uk/programmes/p00gx2dt.

Aitchison, J. (1991, reedited 2012). *Language Change: Progress or Decay?* Cambridge: Cambridge University Press.

Barber, C., Beal, J. & Shaw, P. (2012). *The English Language*. Cambridge: Cambridge University Press.

Cameron, D. (1995). *Verbal Hygiene*. London: Routledge.

Cameron, D. (1997). When Worlds Collide: Expert and Popular Discourse on Language. *The Philosophy of Linguistics: Essays in Honor of Roy Harris* 19 (1): 7–13.

Crystal, D. (1999). Swimming with the tide in a sea of language change. *IATEFL Issues* 149: 2–4.

Crystal, D. (2003). *English as a Global Language*. Cambridge: Cambridge University Press.

Crystal, D. (2004). *The Stories of English*. Woodstock and NY: The Overlook Press.

Culpeper, J. & Nevala, M. (2012). 'Sociocultural processes and the history of English'. In T. Nevalainen & E. Traugott (eds). *The Oxford Handbook of The History of English*. Oxford: Oxford University Press, pp 365–391.

Drummond, R. (2017). Who do you think you're apostrophising? The dark side of grammar pedantry. *The Conversation*. Available at: http://theconversation.com/who-do-you-think-youre-apostrophising-the-dark-side-of-grammar-pedantry-75793.

Eckert, P. (2011). 'Adolescent Language'. In E. Finegan & J.R. Rickford (eds). *Language in the USA*. Cambridge: Cambridge University Press, pp 361–374.

Engel, M. (2017). *That's The Way It Crumbles: The American Conquest of English*. London: Profile Books.

Evans, V. (2017). *The Emoji Code: The Linguistics Behind Smiley Faces and Scaredy Cats*. NY: Picador.

Fairclough, N. (2014). *Language and Power*. London: Routledge.

Giovanelli, M. (2016). *The value of linguistics to the teacher*. In M. Giovanelli & D. Clayton (eds), *Knowing about language: linguistics and the secondary English classroom*. National Association for the Teaching of English (NATE). Abingdon (UK), Routledge. pp. 13–24.

Greene, R.L. (2011). *You Are What You Speak: Grammar Grouches, Language Laws and the Politics of Identity*. NY: Delacorte Press.

Grosjean, F. (2012). *Bilingual: Life and Reality*. Harvard: Harvard University Press.

Gywnne, N. (2013). *Gywnne's Grammar*. London: Random House.

Halliday, M. (2009). *The Essential Halliday*. London: Continuum.

Huddleston, R. & Pullum, G. (2002). *The Cambridge Grammar of the English Language*. Cambridge: Cambridge University Press.

Humphrys, J. (2005). *Lost for Words: The Mangling and Manipulating of the English Language*. London: Hodder.

Jenkins, J. (2006). Current Perspectives on Teaching World Englishes and English as a Lingua Franca. *TESOL Quarterly* (40) 1: 157–181.

Jenkins, J. (2007). *English as a Lingua Franca: Attitude and Identity*. Oxford: Oxford University Press.

Kachru, B. (1988). The sacred cows of English. *English Today* 16: 3–8.

Kerswill, P. (2003). 'Dialect levelling and geographical diffusion in British English'. In D. Britain & J. Cheshire (eds). *Social Dialectology: In Honour of Peter Trudgill*. Amsterdam: John Benjamins, pp 223–243.

Labov, W. (1972). *Sociolinguistic Patterns*. Philadelphia: University of Pennsylvania Press.

Lakoff, G. & Johnson, M. (1980). *Metaphors We Live By*. Chicago: Chicago University Press.

McArthur, T. (1987). The English Languages? *English Today* 11: 9–13.

Mesthrie, R. & Bhatt, R.M. (2008). *World Englishes: The Study of New Linguistic Varieties*. Cambridge: Cambridge University Press.

Milroy, J. (2002). 'The legitimate language: giving a history to English'. In R. Watts & P. Trudgill (eds). *Alternative Histories of English*. (Fourth edition). London: Routledge, pp 7–25.

Nettle, D. & Romaine, S. (2000). *Vanishing Voices: The Extinction of the World's Languages*. Oxford: Oxford University Press.

Phillipson, R. (1992). *Linguistic Imperialism*. Oxford: Oxford University Press.

Pope, R. (1995) *Textual Intervention: Creative and Critical Strategies for Literary Studies*. Oxon: Routledge.

Poussa, P. (1992). 'Pragmatics of *this* and *that*'. In M. Rissanen, I, Ossi, T. Nevalainen & I. Taavitsainen (eds). *History of Englishes: New Methods and Interpretations in Historical Linguistics*. Berlin: Mouton de Gruyter, pp 401–417.

Saraceni, M. (2015). *World Englishes: A Critical Analysis*. London: Bloomsbury.

Sasse, H.J. (1992). 'Theory of language death'. In Brenzinger, M. (ed). *Language Death*. NY: Mouton de Gruyter, pp 7–30.

Schneider, E. (2007). *Postcolonial English: Varieties Around the World*. Cambridge: Cambridge University Press.

Seidlhofer, B. (2011). *Understanding English as a Lingua Franca*. Oxford: Oxford University Press.

Smith, J. (2005). *Essentials of Early English*. London: Routledge.

Simons, G. & Fennig, C. (eds). (2017). *Ethnologue: Languages of the World*. (Twentieth edition). Texas: SIL International. Available at: www.ethnologue.com.

References

Skutnabb-Kangas, T. (1988) 'Multilingualism and the education of minority children'. In Skutnabb-Kangas, T. & Cummins, J. (eds). *Minority Education: From Shame to Struggle*. Clevedon: Multilingual Matters, pp 9–44.

Stenström, A. (2014). *Teenage Talk*. London: Palgrave.

Stuart-Smith, J. & Timmins, C. (2006). "'Tell her to shut her moof': the role of the lexicon in TH-fronting in Glaswegian". In C. Kay, G. Caie, C. Hough & I. Wotherspoon (eds). *The Power of Words: Essays in Lexicography, Lexicology and Semantics: In Honour of Christian J. Kay*. Rodopi: Amsterdam, pp 171–183.

Trask, R.L. (1994). *Language Change*. London: Routledge.

Trask, R.L. (1996). *Historical Linguistics*. London: Routledge.

Truss, L. (2003). *Eats, Shoots and Leaves*. London: Fourth Estate.

Warren, P. (2015). *Uptalk*. Cambridge: Cambridge University Press.

Wolk, L. Abdelli-Beruh, N. & Slavin, D. (2012). Habitual use of vocal fry in young adult female speakers. *Journal of Voice* 26 (3): 111–116.

Glossary

accommodation theory: a sociolinguistic theory arguing that speakers modify their speaking style to become more like or less like the people they are speaking to

acrolect: a prestigious or standard variety of a language

acronym: a process of word formation, whereby the initial letters of a phrase are pronounced as a single word, e.g. NATO for North Atlantic Treaty Organization

adstratum: a type of language contact where there is no dominant language

agreement: the way that word forms correspond to and 'agree' with others

aspiration: the audible breath which may accompany a consonant's articulation. It is marked by a diacritic [ʰ] as in [pʰ]

assimiliation: a process of phonological change, whereby two sounds influence each other and become more alike

basilect: a low prestigious variety of a language

case: a grammatical category related to the morphology of nouns, pronouns, determiners and adjectives, and the role they play in a clause or phrase

chain shift: a situation where a series of sound changes take place, with each one influencing the next

code-switching: when speakers of two (or more) different languages switch from one to the other, often in mid-conversation depending on who they are talking to or what they wish to accomplish. Can also be used to refer to switching between dialects in the same language

computer-mediated communication (CMC): any form of communication that uses the medium of a keyboard or digital device, rather than being spoken or written

conceptual metaphor: a theory of a metaphor whereby one 'domain' of knowledge is 'mapped onto' another domain. The convention for writing conceptual metaphors is through the use of small capitals, in an X IS Y structure

connected speech: a term used to refer to spoken language when analysed in a continuous sequence, including how neighbouring sounds affect one another

corpora: (plural of corpus) large databases of a language, used for research purposes and to document the way that a language is used and changes

corpus linguistics: a method of studying language using computational tools and big datasets (corpora)

covert prestige: where local, vernacular varieties are positively valued in subversive and subconscious ways

Glossary

creole: a language that originally began as a pidgin, and has become the mother-tongue of a speech community, with its own native L1 speakers

Critical Discourse Analysis: an approach to the study of both written and spoken language focusing on the ways that power is enacted

declinist/declinism: a tendency noted by Lane Greene for prescriptivists to view language as being in a state of constant decline from a once great peak

descriptivism: an approach to language study that seeks to describe language use, variation and change, where no judgement or negative attitude is imposed on language

diachronic change: the historical development of language

diglossia: a term mostly used in sociolinguistics, referring to a situation where two very different varieties of a language exist alongside each other, each holding a distinct social function

EFL: English as a Foreign Language, where English is taught as an L2 in schools

elision: a process of phonological change, whereby a sound becomes omitted

emoji: a term to describe visual icons (representations of facial expressions, actions and objects) used in social media messaging

etymology: the study of the origin of words and the way they change in meaning

fortition: a process of phonological change, whereby a sound becomes 'stronger' in its articulation

gender: a grammatical or semantic category of words, showing contrast between masculine, feminine or neuter

global language: a language that holds a 'special role' that is widely recognised in a high number of countries around the world

hypercorrection: an over-emphasis shift in linguistic register, usually when a speaker of a non-standard variety goes 'too far' in trying to emulate the standard variety

initialism: a process of word formation, whereby the initial letters of a phrase are pronounced as separate sounds, e.g. BBC

L1: a speaker's first language

L2: a speaker's second language

language contact: a process of language change whereby multiple languages come into social contact and have linguistic influence on each other, in the form of borrowings, grammatical and phonological change, formation of pidgins and creoles, and higher rates of bilingualism

language shift: a term used to describe a speaker's / speech community's sudden or gradual shift from the use of one language to another

lenition: a process of phonological change, whereby a sound becomes 'weaker' in its articulation

lexical diffusion: the increased use of a linguistic form throughout an area over a period of time

lingua franca: a language used as a contact language between speakers of different first languages

Language change

linguicism: a term used to draw parallels between hierarchies on the basis of race or ethnicity, gender and language

linguistic imperialism: an ideological view and process of language change, whereby one language is imposed on speakers who use another language, often undermining the rights of those speakers. It promotes the idea that there is a hierarchy of languages

linguistic purism: a pejorative label used for a view that sees a language as needing preservation from things that might make it change, such as dialect variation and borrowings from other languages

mesolect: an intermediate prestigious variety of a language

metaphor: the use of figurative language, where one thing is understood in terms of another thing

mood/modality: a system of meaning related to a speaker's attitude to, confidence in, or perception about something in the world

multi-modal communication: a way of communicating that uses multiple channels (e.g. speech and body language)

number: grammatical marking indicating whether a word is in the singular or plural form

official language: a language used by a country in settings such as government, the legal courts, the media and education. Some countries recognise multiple official languages

overt prestige: where varieties to be valued are publicly and explicitly recommended by powerful institutions and social groups, and are seen as socially desirable

peace linguistics: an approach to linguistics that emphasises the value of language diversity and the need to respect the dignity of individual speakers and speech communities

pidgin: a language that develops between two speech communities who do not share a common language

prescriptivism: the notion that language should be fixed, prescribing to a set standard of rules for language usage, with any shift away from these rules or standards being seen as incorrect

register: a particular variety of language as defined according to the way it is used in social situations and different contexts – for example, a register of formal English; a register of business English, etc.

rising intonation: using a rising tone as an utterance ends. Generally used when asking a question, but now more prevalent in statements. Can also be referred to as high-rising terminals or uptalk

sociophonetics: a branch of linguistics at the interface of sociolinguistics and phonetics

speech community: any socially or regionally defined group in which its members share a number of linguistic characteristics

standardisation: the process under which a language develops a standard 'prestige' variety

substratum: a type of language contact where the language of a less powerful group influences the language of a more powerful group

Glossary

superstratum: a type of language contact where the language of a more powerful group influences the language of a less powerful group

synchronic change: the study of language change at a particular moment in time

tap (flap): a manner of articulation of consonant sounds, whereby a single, rapid point of contact is made between two vocal articulators (such as the tongue and the roof of the mouth)

th-fronting: a phonological process whereby the dental fricatives /θ/ and /ð/ shift forward in the mouth to a labio-dental fricative of /f/ or /v/ sound, respectively

vocal fry/creaky voice: a way of speaking that constricts the vocal folds and creates a creaking, low frequency sound

writing system: a method for visually representing spoken language, including letters of alphabets and punctuation marks

Index

Page numbers in italics are figures; with 't' are tables.

Americanisms 73–4, *73*
assimilation 45–6
attitudes to change 60
  description 3–4, 64–7
  lexical change 73–7, *73*, 75–6t
  and metaphors 67–70
  and phonological change 70–2
  prescription 4, 60–7

borrowing 40–1, *41*

causes of change 55–7
change, defined 10–11
code-switching 7, 8
Critical Discourse Analysis (CDA) 60

death, language 97–100, *99*
description 3–4, 64–7

emoji use 74–7, 75–6t
endangerment, language 97–100, *99*

fortition 47–8

global languages 81, 100–1
grammar 51–5, 52–4t, 60
Great Vowel Shift 29, *29–30*

history of English 14
  Old English 14–16, *16–17*, 17–22
  Middle English 22–7
  Early Modern English 27–30, *29*

Late Modern English 30–1, *32*
Present Day English (PDE) 32–4

identity 7, 22, 25, 30, 48, 52, 60, 65–6, 89-90, 95, 101, 108
ideologies 60

language contact 92–5
language shift 98, *99*
lenition 46–7, *46*
lexical change 39–43, *41*, 73–7, 75–6t
lingua franca 93–4

McArthur's circle of World Englishes 87–8, *88*
metaphors 8–10, *9*, 44, 67–70, 77
morphological change 55
Multicultural London English (MLE) 50–1

phonological change 45–51, *49*, 70–2
pidgins/creoles 15, *88*, 95–6
politics 60
prescription 4, 60–7
prestige, and classifying varieties of English 89–90, *90–1*
printing 28–9

Queen's English Society (QES) 52, 52–4t, 54, 69

register 66–7
rising intonation 72

Schneider's dynamic model 88–9
semantic change 43–5
social function of language 2–3, *3*, 5–8, 5–6t
sociophonetics 48–51, *49*
speech communities 5–6
speech forms, continuum 91, *91*
standardisation 27
studies of language change 3–10, 37–9, *38*

technology 5, 27, 28, 30–1, 32, 43, 74–7, 75–6t
three circles model 86–7, *86*

vocal fry 70–1
vowel reduction 47

word formation 41–3
world Englishes 84–91, *86*, *88*, *90–1*
  defined 81–4, *82*, *84–5*
  and global languages 100–1
  and language contact 92–5
language endangerment/death 97–100, *99*
pidgins/creoles 15, *88*, 95–6

Acknowledgements

The authors and publishers acknowledge the following sources of copyright material and are grateful for the permissions granted. While every effort has been made, it has not always been possible to identify the sources of all the material used, or to trace all copyright holders. If any omissions are brought to our notice, we will be happy to include the appropriate acknowledgements on reprinting.

Development of this publication has made use of the Cambridge English Corpus (CEC). The CEC is a multi-billion word computer database of contemporary spoken and written English. It includes British English, American English and other varieties of English. It also includes the Cambridge Learner Corpus, developed in collaboration with Cambridge English Language Assessment. Cambridge University Press has built up the CEC to provide evidence about language use that helps to produce better language teaching materials.

Thanks to the following for permission to reproduce images:

Cover image: Stephen Dorey/Getty Images

Chapter 1 Westend61/Getty Images; Chapter 2 Richard Baker/In Pictures via Getty Images; Fig. 2.2 CM Dixon/Print Collector/Getty Images; Fig. 2.3 Paul Fearn/Alamy Stock Photo; Chapter 3 Vanessa Davies/Getty Images; Fig. 3.2 Google Books Ngram Viewer http://books.google.com/ngrams; Chapter 4 Amith Nag Photography/Getty Images; within Fig. 4.1 yayayoyo/Getty Images; Chapter 5 monkeybusinessimages/Getty Images; Fig. 5.2 & 5.7 Ian Cushing; Fig. 5.3 Cultura RF/Seb Oliver/Getty Images; Fig. 5.4 map 'English as an international language: Directions in the 1990s' by Peter Strevens, first appeared in *English Teaching Forum*, October 1987

The publisher would like to thank the following members of The Cambridge Panel: English who assisted in reviewing this book: Anisa Kavat, Carolin Haubold and Angela Janovsky